West Monroe
BACKWOODS

Ron Coody

SOME SPECIAL FOLKS

As you read through these stories you'll realize pretty quickly that it was written in part to honor some special people in our lives who have moved on. My hearty pioneer grandparents Pawpaw and Mawmaw exemplified a love for a simple lifestyle, animals and their family members. We miss my sister Carrie's bubbly personality. Daddy was one of a kind and without his love for the backwoods this story wouldn't have happened.

CONTENTS

ACKNOWLEDGMENTS

I want to thank my wife Jean for her patience during yet
another book. I love having her at my side in all the
backwoods outings around the world. Our five boys have
given me great inspiration for looking at things in a new way.
I wish them many adventures in the backwoods. Momma
kept correcting my grammar, so that the words coming out of
my mouth and through my fingers at least make sense some
of the time. Thank you all.

"IF A MAN DOES NOT KEEP PACE WITH HIS COMPANIONS, PERHAPS IT IS BECAUSE HE HEARS A DIFFERENT DRUMMER. LET HIM STEP TO THE MUSIC WHICH HE HEARS, HOWEVER MEASURED OR FAR AWAY"

HENRY DAVID THOREAU

STEP INTO THE BACKWOODS

More than ducks lurk in the Louisiana backwoods. All kinds of strange and secretive critters live out their wild lives in the bayous and by-ways, pine groves and hardwood bottoms, creeping around on the squishy ground that never seems to completely dry up, even in the baking hot summers. Crazy coons and gawking gators, silly squirrels and proud bucks are just a few of the local residents. The less popular among them include the deadly poisonous water moccasin, or as it's fondly called, the "cotton mouth." Misleading name. Not much cottony or cozy about those inch-long fangs dripping with venom. The strong and colorful wild turkeys don't mind the snakes much since they live 10 to 15 feet above the forest floor in their hickory or holly perches.

The list of wild things goes on and on, but this isn't mainly their story. The deep delta backwoods have provided a home to people since nearly the dawn of time. While the seasons faithfully change from summer's oppressive humidity to autumn's blue skies, then to winter's penetrating chill and finally spring's eruption of tantalizing scents and irresistible babies in their burrows, Louisiana families like mine do what we do best...enjoy the zest of life.

Since growing up in West Monroe I've come to gain a new appreciation for the backwoods ways of life. As an adult my work has carried me all over the world. I've gone to places that could just as well have been in another solar system when I was a kid, they were that far away and different from the protected patch of wetlands behind our house on Tupawek bayou. While the success of Duck Dynasty's Robertson family has brought unbelievable global attention to the sleepy town of West Monroe, it has also reminded many of us natives just how good we have it. Sometimes it takes an outside look to make you glad for what you've got.

And in fact we've got a lot. Lots of woods, lots of wildlife, lots of history, lots of delicious food, lots of memories and lots of stories. Louisiana gives a backdrop for a few of these tales from the backwoods. Pour yourself a tall glass of ice tea, turn down the fire on your turnip greens and get your waders on for a long walk into the West Monroe Backwoods.

"POVERTY POINT
IS LOUISIANA'S TAJ MAHAL"

--THE TIMES SHREVEPORT

A REALLY BIG PILE OF DIRT

Poverty Point? Is this the name of a new shopping mall? No one knows for sure. Maybe it was a shopping mall a long time ago. The mother of all malls. It was big enough and had ample room for parking, if anyone had bothered to invent the wheel back then, which they didn't. But who needed wheels when waterways surrounded you on all sides? Just build a boat, or a raft, or grab a log or just jump in and swim. You'll eventually wind up somewhere, if you can get past the floating stumps and other driftwood.

Thousands of years back Native American tribes mastered the waterways, using the great Mississippi River, the Red River, the Ohio and countless other tributaries for trade and survival. They could drop a canoe in the White River north of present day Indianapolis and with enough time, energy and good weather, paddle up the Ouachita River into West Monroe. When the French fur traders later came up from New Orleans, they learned invaluable backwater skills from the experienced Indians.

But long before the New World was even a twinkle in Columbus' eye, the annual cycle of spring flooding in the Mississippi delta forced the people to regularly seek higher ground. That was a problem though. If you go too far from the high ground, you can't very easily get in a good day of fishing. Maybe for this reason, or some other mysterious one we'll never know, the ancient people living along the bayous and streams decided to make their own hills.

If being old means being important, then the oldest of these backwoods Louisiana mounds is very, very important. Found just south of West Monroe on the west bank of Watson Brake, this little collection of mounds is about 5400 years old. Just how old is that? It was old when the pyramids were built. It's the oldest structure in the Western hemisphere. Whatever else that means, it says that people have been fishing and hunting in the West Monroe backwoods for a long, long time!

Over by the Mississippi River, where big-time game occupied a massive wilderness that sat nearly half the year under water, some other Indian settlers got really busy. Their big pile of dirt made all the others look like fire ant hills. Coming along nearly 2000 years after the Watson Brake builders, these guys showed some real industry. When they put the finishing touches on what would become known as the Poverty Point mounds, they might have smiled had they known the future. The hundred-foot tall bird-shaped mound, surrounded by shorter mounds laid out like an amphitheater, was the largest ever built in North America. They dug in the swampy soil with simple tools and weed baskets. They had no Wal-Mart down the highway to pick up a fresh bar of soap and a frozen pizza. Considering that Louisiana mud has a consistency somewhat between a bowl of cold grits and wet cement, their feat of engineering is astounding.

In 2013 the venerable Poverty Point mounds got a respectable promotion. It's now a World Heritage Site. That puts among the elite. There are only 22 in the US. Stonehenge and the Pyramids of Giza have the same honor. But giving it a new name doesn't change what obvious to the honest visitor. It's still just a really big pile of dirt.

"NOT ALL THOSE WHO WANDER ARE LOST."

-- *J.R.R. TOLKIEN, THE FELLOWSHIP OF THE*

RING

OUR FIRST HIKE WITH DADDY

In the late 1960's Daddy was robust and trim. He served in WW2 with the Navy on a surveillance blimp, keeping an eye on the Caribbean for Nazi submarines. After the war, the GI Bill granted him a free college education. He studied accounting at Louisiana Tech, which is just a thirty mile drive from West Monroe through the piney hills. With much of the North Louisiana economy based on the backwoods logging industry, it was no big surprise that after graduation he landed a job at the West Monroe paper mill south of I-20 in the redneck neighborhood of Bawcomville.

Shopping around for a good place to build a home and raise a family, Momma and Daddy settled on a heavily wooded lot outside the West Monroe city limits where a rugged old Southern landowner decided to break up his farmland. Two or three branches of the upper Tupawek bayou flow through the area, draining the west Ouachita Parish highland. The creeks eventually join together in a snake-like ribbon, cutting out deep gullies before blessing the Ouachita River with a little more water.

When Momma and Daddy toured the available lots, they found plenty of choices. Each one had trees thicker than the hair on a hound dog. Enough time had passed since loggers and settlers had cleared the original timber to allow a healthy stand of new growth. Pines, hickories, oaks, sweetgums and many other species flourished in the rich soil on the hillsides, watered by the abundant creeks. The developer dammed up two of the creeks to create small ponds. But the overflow kept the creeks regularly supplied. They looked over the forests and hills and creeks and came to a decision. They picked a piece of land with the right amount of level ground for a front yard and then a spacious backyard that first sloped gently and then rather sharply down to the creek. At the bottom of the hill countless rains had sculpted a winding creek couched in a flat floodplain.

A carpenter friend from church built them a sturdy little brick house at the top of the hill several years before I was born. Like homesteaders, they continually cut and cleared, cut and cleared, burning piles of underbrush in an attempt to tame the woods. By the time I arrived several years after my older sisters Vicki and Carrie, you couldn't exactly call their yard the "backwoods", at least not near the house. But as you made your way down the hill to the heavily wooded creek at the bottom, if you listened carefully you could still hear the call of the wild.

Vicki and Carrie heard the call and loved playing at the wood's edge. Daddy built a footbridge that opened new horizons for adventure under the dark canopy. He also built a tall wooden fence—more like a wall—that marked the boundary between civilization and nature. It showed how far they had conquered and that there is a limit to all perfection.

After joining the family, I gazed down the hill at the distant red fence and beyond, to the immense assortment of greens and grays that made up the forest roof. The trees in Louisiana grow much taller than in many other parts of the US. To my young mind the great span of the oak branches and towering pine trunks seemed to touch heaven itself. How I wanted to explore the backwoods!

One Saturday morning my dream came true. "Let's go on a hike," Daddy said. "It's a fine day."

The day was good. Cool weather had greatly scaled back the poison ivy, poison snakes and redbugs. I was still very little, but my big sisters, one nine years older and one seven, were eager to take Daddy's suggestion and get us organized. They enjoyed lots more freedom than I did when it came to crossing the creek into the woods where a thick carpet of pine needles made a magical fairy land for them and their neighbor friends to play hide and seek and build little forts.

"I'll make sandwiches," one of my sisters offered. "We can pack them and have a real hike."

"Alright, that sounds like a fine idea," Daddy said with a smile. He was a soft-spoken Southern gentleman who sometimes was mistaken for Richard Nixon and talked a bit like Andy Griffith.

My sisters quickly got our supplies ready for the big excursion. I felt elated. With my father leading the way and both of my sisters armed with backwoods savvy I anticipated a true adventure. Down the hill we flew, across the bridge and into the woods. But this time we wouldn't quickly turn back. Daddy took us past the thick pine carpet near the woods edge and up the hillside ahead. Annoyed blue-jays scolded us from their perches in the oaks, squirrels nervously rushed back and forth in the high branches and we tried to keep our eyes wide open for any stubborn snakes still out braving the cold. We skirted the steep hill overlooking the creek below, making our way upwards toward a small feeder branch of the creek. This little creek rarely had water, making it easy for us to scour the sand and gravel for treasures.

Pressing onward we started the steep ascent across a field of armadillo holes. Rotting logs and limbs lay strewn amongst the holes. We stumbled and struggled through the rough terrain, having to pull ourselves free from briars and thorny vines that tenaciously clung to the tree bark on one side and us on the other. This was the real backwoods and I relished every sound of the wildlife and smell of the plants and soil.

Our little band of explorers blazed through the unknown until we reached the trail's end. A rusty barb-wire fence abruptly jutted up from the ground. Partly rotted wooden posts managed to keep three homely barb-wire strands off the ground. The fence ran around a partly woody field, probably left over from some cattle farming years earlier. No livestock of any kind remained, but some huge oak trees soared skyward with their branches displayed like the top of a cathedral.

"Let's eat our lunch," Vicki said.

"Yeah, this is a good place," Carrie replied.

Daddy gazed at the majestic oaks. "Yes, sir," he said, "that's a good idea."

We popped the pack open. Food always tastes different when you eat it outside in the fresh air. It's more real somehow, with more flavor. Those sandwiches didn't disappoint. With new energy we pulled and pushed our way through more briar thickets lining the fence and then gradually hiked down the hill back to the creek. Still a small boy, I felt quite tired when we reached the bridge. I turned to look into the woods again. The afternoon dampness made the air feel cooler. Shadows were growing longer with the sun slowly dropping in the western sky.

My sister said, "That was fun, Daddy, thank you."

"You're welcome, that was real nice," he said, turning to walk up the hill to the house.

I was thankful too, but much too fascinated with the forest to say or notice anything else. I had seen a glimpse of the backwoods. In spite of thorns and barb-wire fences, for me it was a glimpse of freedom.

"TWO ROADS DIVERGED IN A WOOD, AND
I—
I TOOK THE ONE LESS TRAVELED BY,
AND THAT HAS MADE ALL THE
DIFFERENCE. "

-- ROBERT FROST

THREE NAME PARK

No, the biggest park in West Monroe is not named after a lost Indian tribe. Before the dawn of the suburb, the steep gullies and deep swamps found along the wandering Tupawek Bayou provided a wonderland for fascinating exploration. Some local businessmen and leaders with foresight realized that part of the land should be preserved and enjoyed. So three service groups, the Kiwanis, Rotary and Lions teamed up to create Ki-ro-li Park. Each group donated not only money and service, but gave part of their name to the new park which the Boy Scouts used for years.

Knowing the true story didn't stop me from imagining more exotic origins for the beautiful park with its proud pine trees and gnarly cypress knees. When I was still pretty young, word went through town that West Monroe had purchased the park from the Boy Scouts and would turn it into a recreation center, complete with tennis courts, hiking trails and scenic overlooks. I couldn't wait for Daddy to drive us on the winding road through the woods over to Kiroli. What secrets would it hold? Maybe hunting trails that the Native Americans followed in search of game? Hidden fishing holes where they caught the biggest catfish for their feasts and celebrations? My childhood imagination took me farther back into a fantastic world, where little forest people like elves and dwarves danced under the eerie vines in the moon's full light.

The grand opening for Kiroli came one Sunday afternoon.

"When are we going, Daddy?" I asked the question several times before we could get our lunch down. We always had a big meal after church, but I was in no mood to linger over it.

"What's that?" he said, with something else obviously on his mind. Daddy's mind rarely went into neutral. Computer technology had just started to develop and I knew he was probably mulling over some problem from the paper mill. But the grand opening of Kiroli was simply too important to miss.

"We should get ready to go," I insisted. "Kiroli opens this afternoon."

"That's right! Let's get going" he said, pushing back his lunch plate.

"You be careful." Momma said. Then she added, "And don't forget I need to be at choir practice by 5:30."

Her urgings to drive safely were never unnecessary. I always felt a bit nervous whenever I had to ride in Daddy's huge sedan. Even though it was roughly the size, shape and weight of a Sherman tank, his habit of getting distracted while trying to mentally work out an accounting problem definitely put him in the high risk driver category.

At least we didn't have far to go. The creek that went through our back yard was the same one that flowed through Kiroli not more than a mile or two downstream. Daddy pulled the heavy car onto Arkansas road and wound his way along with me anxiously hoping he was watching those two double yellow lines in the middle. He must have been paying attention because we got to Kiroli Park in good order.

West Monroe acquired the park in a primitive state. Someone had stuck an unused railroad caboose in the woods off to the left of the road. Instead of grass, dust covered most of the open areas. The footpaths could hardly be distinguished from the forest floor. Green duckweed covered much of the two small lakes bordering the park on the west. A few tattered bunkhouses showed that the Boy Scouts had once used the park for camping, but they didn't look fit now even for the few spiders and field mice hiding in their corners. A big welcome sign hung between a couple of friendly trees. So this was the grand opening?

Nevertheless, while I walked around under the pines and peered down into the deep Tupawek swamp, a feeling of longing for more of the backwoods started creeping into my bones. What would it feel like to fly unfettered among the treetops like the red-headed woodpecker, landing in a split-second on the bark to eat the choicest beetles? How does the mother raccoon feel when her little ones snuggle down in a soft den halfway up an ancient tree trunk? What makes the frogs sing such weird songs when the moon rises?

We walked and talked until we grew tired and the time had come to get Momma to choir practice. In the years following that first visit, the people of West Monroe invested thousands more dollars and hours transforming Kiroli into a place where the local residents, human and otherwise, could live in peace...our little Eden.

"THE GROSS HEATHENISM OF
CIVILIZATION HAS GENERALLY
DESTROYED NATURE, AND POETRY, AND
ALL THAT IS SPIRITUAL."

-- JOHN MUIR

PLAYING HOOKY WITH THE TEACHER

Halfway between Kiroli and downtown West Monroe stands the little elementary school called Highland. Honestly, in the years since attending there through sixth grade, I have forgotten an awful lot. That probably wouldn't surprise some of my teachers, who could see that trying to put a hyperactive kid like me into a hard wooden desk for 8 hours and telling him to be absolutely quiet was about as smart as putting two raccoons in the same bag of trash. My second grade teacher Mrs. Robbins had an inspiration to paint a green spot for me on the front step of the school house. I was strictly instructed to sit on that green spot after school while waiting for my mother to come pick me up. That's just what I wanted; after sitting all day in a hard wooden desk, I was forced yet once again to sit, this time on cold cement!

They meant well, I'm sure. Mrs. Robbins always prayed before we went to lunch, "God is Great, God is good, let us thank him for this food, Amen." Before anyone gets bent out of shape, they should know she doesn't teach there anymore. I suspect that where she is now, she's among the kind of folk who still appreciate prayer in school.

One glorious school day something unforgettable happened to break through the monotony. It might have been Mrs. Robbins, or perhaps my first grade teacher Mrs. Moffit, or yet someone else. I'm not sure who had the idea, but I believe it's worth sharing here.

Our class of twenty or so busy, fidgeting little West Monroe baby-boomers, freshly scrubbed by their loving parents, sat feeling bored and distracted on a beautiful spring day. The pale green government-issue paint on the walls might as well have been made in the Soviet Union, it was so blah-looking. We had a few colors around the classroom in the form of the American flag, a springtime bulletin board and some assorted pictures. But when we looked out the windows, the azure sky, the piney evergreen and movement of buzzing bees made everything inside all the more boring. Our discerning teacher could see when to raise the white flag of surrender.

"Okay class, today we will do something special," she said.

The perkiness in her voice got our attention.

"I want everyone to listen closely to my instructions. We are going on a little field trip. Everyone has to stay close together and mind me."

A mummer rippled through the room.

"You have to stay in line and everyone will walk together.

We're going to see some of the things we've been talking about in class. Pay special attention to the plants and trees and bugs. It's a beautiful day and I think we'll all enjoy it."

The classroom started to buzz with voices. Here was a chance. Escape from captivity. Even the most bookish among us couldn't help but feel happy about this interruption to our daily grind. We lined up at the door and then filed down the long straight corridor. Kids whispered and poked each other in excitement. We stole glances into other classrooms, gloating over the other boys and girls still trapped in the heartless prison system. We were free and going out of the school. It was so wonderful we could hardly believe our good fortune.

Our teacher led us past the office, giving a word or two at the front desk. Then it was through the double doors and into the wider world. Of course we had recesses every day in a rather expansive playground where we could run madly and scream off our silly heads. But this was different at the deepest level. This jaunt took us off the school grounds altogether, away from the carefully manicured government property.

"Everyone still together? Stay in line and don't talk too much. I want you to look around and see what there is."

That was one instruction I didn't need. My eyes had already widened with wonder, soaking in everything that assailed my senses. Spring in Louisiana brings a cloud of natural aromas. The warmth and humidity capture the smells better than a bottle of French perfume.

A squirrel chattered at us from someone's yard. Though Highland wasn't in the woods, the homes next to it had a wide array of both domestic and wild growth. We walked along the roadside across from the school, pointing at unusual flowers, looking up into the treetops for fat squirrels and occasionally poking or shoving each other in our glee at being set free from the cold classroom.

"Okay, here's a very pretty garden behind this house," our teacher said, motioning to the left. "I want you all to look around, tell me what you notice."

"That squirrel is making a funny noise," a little girl said.

"He's mad at us," a boy replied.

"We have lots of those in our yard," another boy added.

"That's good, what else do you see?" she said. "Look at these vines on the fence, these are honeysuckle. Here, let's smell them. See how sweet they are."

I took a big sniff. They did smell wonderful. Too bad I couldn't get my mother some in a bottle, since she enjoyed nice perfumes.

"Okay, everyone back in line, time to go now," our teacher said, motioning us to line up again.

We quietly obeyed. It was hard to turn back but the outdoors gave us renewed contentment. We lined up and walked to the school building and down the hall. That short field trip changed our outlook. Maybe it was a small change, maybe it was much more. Just stepping outside the boundaries of the government green paint and touching nature's evergreen for those few precious minutes widened our horizons. The world was now our classroom.

"I LOVE TO LIVE ON THE BRINK OF ETERNITY.
MAY I NEVER LOITER IN MY HEAVENLY
JOURNEY."

-- DAVID BRAINERD

MASON JARS AND ARROWHEADS

Our ancestors first came to Louisiana from the east. Genealogy records indicate that some folks by the name of Coode might have originated in Cornwall, England, not far from King Arthur's castle Camelot. In America they changed the spelling to Coody, giving it a modern look. Well, it was modern for 1780. These days it has the misfortune of sounding like *Cooties*, the school yard game where kids infect one another with a pesky invisible bug. I prefer the Camelot version of the name.

Once in the New World, the Coodys found wives, sometimes among the Cherokees of Appalachia, had lots of kids and moved around many times. They apparently didn't care too much for cold weather, maybe because they came from southern England, so when they moved, they went south. Tennessee and Georgia made good homes, but some wanted more space, so they drifted into north Louisiana. On my mother's side of the family--the Wright side (some would argue it's the *right* side)--some hearty pioneers also planted their roots in the Mississippi delta. One thing led to another as it always happens, and the Coodys and Wrights became in-laws. With seven boys, a restless nature and the Great Depression, Grandfather Coody didn't manage to keep any ancestral land in the family. But Pawpaw Wright stayed put and worked hard to keep ownership of his family's homestead that dated back to the 1840s. It's an 80-acre spread of land that rises slightly above the Boeuf River in West Carroll Parish.

Once or twice each month, we loaded up the family car and drove out of West Monroe eastward to the homestead. My mother was born in a simple cypress-plank cabin built at the highest point on the farm. She and her younger brother helped their parents scatter the chicken feed, slop the pigs, gather the purple-hull peas, scrub the kitchen floor, mend the clothes, water the horses and clean the fish. Their self-sufficiency and hard work sustained several generations of pioneers through even the toughest days of the 1927 flood and the Great Depression.

Pawpaw thought it was good for us kids to get out of the "city" and spend time on the farm. I hardly considered myself a city-dweller. I could dive into the backwoods behind our house and not emerge for hours without stepping in the same mudhole twice. But this was different. This was a real homestead, the real frontier. Before telephones arrived the nearest neighbors were so far away they could only be reached by ringing a big bell on a tower in the front yard. Their working farm depended on animals and gardens for survival, not just entertainment. Antebellum West Carroll didn't have wealthy plantations with privileged gentry and slaves. The handful of people scattered across the parish lived without much money and yet gave generously to help out their fellow man.

"Hi there, Sugar," Pawpaw said, welcoming all of us grandkids at the front door with a big hug. He always called us Sugar, though I'm certain it was an act of faith. Mawmaw usually stood in the background, quietly beaming at us before slipping back in the kitchen to stir a pot of boiling turnips and batter the fish.

They lived in a quaint little farmhouse Pawpaw built on the front end of the homestead. The original farmhouse, made of weathered cypress boards cut from virgin timber, stood out back and now housed cows and bulls instead of people. He also had a couple of other barns, a large henhouse, some sheds scattered around the pastures for hogs and cattle, roughhewn wooden feeding troughs for the hungry crowds of critters and several shade trees on the west side of the house where we could sit and chew the fat in the cool of the evening. Fences made of salvaged cypress boards merged with newer barb-wire to keep the different animals sectioned off in their own grazing areas. The hogs enjoyed a big pasture on the west complete with a shady patch of bodock trees under which they wallowed in a perpetually wet pool of mud. If there was ever a real "hog heaven," their spot out in the pasture was the place.

So much happened on the old farm place, we'll have to come back to it later for other stories. But one very important point should be made at the outset. Like Poverty Point and Watson Brake, the homestead history ran deep in the soil…literally. I learned that at an early age.

"Ronnie, come here, I want to show you something," Mawmaw said, calling me from the kitchen.

Her kitchen smelled the best in the world. She used hand-churned butter from her own cows to make fresh rolls and biscuits. The catfish and buffalo fish came out of the Boeuf River, usually delivered by a neighbor who had plenty to spare. Sweet corn and ripe red tomatoes grew in the garden. I ran to the kitchen savoring the smells. "Yes Ma'am?"

Mawmaw was a slight woman. She had never been very large, but health problems and hard farm life slowed her down. She moved to the kitchen cabinet. With great curiosity I watched her gingerly remove a Mason jar from the shelf. "Here it is. See what I found in the potato patch last week?"

She put her hand down in the jar. I strained to get a better look.

"What is it?" I asked, getting closer to inspect the strange object.

Mawmaw loved children. Her love showed all the years she taught Sunday school at the little country church in Goodwill. She could see on my face now that I was hooked. "It's an arrowhead," she answered. "I found it in the dirt when I was digging up potatoes."

"A real arrowhead! From your garden?!" Before she could say any more I tore out the kitchen to the boot and hat room containing a wide assortment of their outdoor gear. This was simply too good to pass up. Treasures, right there in the ground. I had no time to waste. "I'm going to find more."

Wearing Pawpaw's straw hat and wading boots I trudged through the tall grass in the pasture past the sagging cypress barn and up a slight rise in the land to the vegetable patch, climbing over a fence here and there and trying to avoid stepping in the cow patties. The garden was an acre or two, just a small corner on the big 40 acres of cotton he grew. But boy, it could produce. I wasn't concerned with vegetables though, I had serious business locating ancient artifacts. Up and down the rows I slowly walked, my eyes scanning the big chunks of dirt kicked up by a recent plowing. A fleck of color caught my eye. Too bad, just a red potato bug, dead in the dirt. I had no end of patience for a task this important. Back and forth I looked, leaving no dirt clod unturned, no potato undisturbed. If no arrowheads turned up my first day as an avid archeologist, the lack of success only enflamed my determination for the next time.

As with all things in Louisiana, the weather was the final arbiter in deciding our daily plans. Each visit to the farm I eagerly watched the cotton and rice fields for cues about the condition of the ground. Too much rain meant too much mud and that meant sinking in the garden up to my neck. Someone would have to dig me out instead of an arrowhead. Too much sun meant too little moisture and that meant I would be walking on cemented soil. But then I had those Goldilocks days when everything was just right.

On such a day I carefully worked my way up a long plow-row, stirring up a little dust by kicking open large dirt clods. It was warm and I was getting tired. Then I saw it. Partly exposed in a dirt clod on top of the furrow, a purplish rock caught my eye. Pawpaw's oversized boots flopped on my feet, nearly tripping me as I hopped over dirt clods and decaying plant stalks. My heart pounded with excitement when I saw there was no mistake. An arrowhead made of smooth purple flint jutted up at me.

With the new found arrowhead in my pocket I ran as fast as the floppy boots, long grass and cow patties would allow, about to burst with the news of my success. Mawmaw welcomed me with a huge smile and a kind word of affirmation.

My driving hunger to find more arrowheads would subside, probably about the same time my interest in girls shifted into high gear. But by then I had amassed a pretty decent collection of arrowheads, stone tools and flint chips I found in the garden and given to me from kind friends of the family. A simple hobby? Yes, I suppose. But for me Mawmaw's well-used Mason jar and that first arrowhead shed light on both life's permanence and transience.

"CAJUN COOKING IS THE
ABILITY TO TAKE WHAT YOU HAVE AND
CREATE A GOOD DISH AND SEASON IT
RIGHT…I GHA-RAWN-TEE!"

-- *JUSTIN WILSON*

IS THAT PEGGY OR P G?

There's a pretty basic rule about speaking correctly when you visit West Monroe. If you're not from around here, you'll probably mispronounce everything. Get used to it.

When we wrapped up a scorching hot day at Mawmaw and Pawpaw's picking purple hull peas, cleaning freshly caught catfish and helping out with other farm chores, we piled into the family car with two important destinations in mind. Neither one was our kitchen in West Monroe. The first destination was the corner ice cream shop in Mer Rouge, about half way home. The second was PeGes, just off Bayou Desiard in Monroe. Now go ahead, get it out of your system, try to say these names correctly. Okay, I'm all ears. That's what I thought, you mispronounced every one. No problem, we still love you anyway and we'll save you a spot at PeGes where you can enjoy the best Po'boys this side of Bourbon Street.

In the steaming afternoon the car air conditioning did its best, but even at that we barely made it the twenty mile stretch of highway across the Kennedy rice plantation west of the Boeuf. All eyes strained to see ahead when we saw an occasional farmhouse, signaling that Mer Rouge was getting close. Just a little farther and we'd see the tip-top of the Kennedy grain elevators next to the Mer Rouge train track. Then came the John Deere dealer, the hundred-year-old Episcopal Church and finally-- Praise the Lord!--across the tracks, the Mer Rouge ice cream shop.

Not stopping was completely out of the question. That would be akin to suggesting we skip Christmas or become school drop-outs. This little hamlet, with a peculiar mixture of wealth and poverty, Antebellum South and Happy Days America, was the home of, to put it bluntly, the best ice cream on the planet. We never figured out their secret recipe. It had the chocolatiest chocolate and creamiest vanilla, with the slightest hint of saltiness and a perfect balance between smooth and icy in its texture. As to sweetness and consistency, it was just enough sugar to fire up the blood and just firm enough to be faithful to its cone for several minutes in a baking 100 degrees.

With inexpressible elation we received our Mer Rouge ice cream. It quieted down the most agitated traveler among us during the long drive across the disgusting "wham brake", or as it was also called, "stink creek", and through the piney uplands outside of Bastrop. That brought us to the outskirts of Monroe and to the next very important, if not essential, roadside stop. Rays PeGe.

West Monroe and Monroe are called the Twin Cities. It's an odd designation, since they don't resemble one another in the slightest. The only thing they have in common, besides both being in Louisiana, is four bridges: the Louisville Bridge, the railroad bridge, the I-20 Bridge and another generic bridge that really should be sealed off and used for a skateboard park or mini-putt. Monroe has the Garden District, Neville High School, University of Louisiana-Monroe (formerly Northeast Louisiana University, but name changed to make no mistake it is really in Monroe), Louisiana Purchase Gardens and Zoo, the Biedenharn Center with an outstanding Bible collection and Coca-Cola Museum, a regional airport, Pecanland shopping mall…in short, Monroe has it all. It's several times bigger than West Monroe, used to have its own power plant and golf course and still has a courthouse and civic center and so on and so forth and what not. That's all well and good and folks from West Monroe don't mind occasionally driving over the bridges—except the peculiar one that should be used for skateboards—so they can shop and dine out and watch Louisiana Tech beat ULM in sports and West Monroe High School beat every other football team in the universe into oblivion.

Before I lose any Monroe readers here, let me just say that West Monroe realizes that it doesn't have the really fancy historical houses, the founder of Coca-Cola and Delta airlines, a national university, a big shopping mall and well, you get my drift. Many Monroe folks have excelled in education and entrepreneurism and you got to respect them for that.

What West Monroe does have is hard-working folks, many of whom keep the mighty presses at the paper mill turning day and night and many others who faithfully serve in a wide variety of vocations. Some of these folks could be called rednecks, and not a few, like myself, would prefer to wear such a name as a title

41

of honor. Because a redneck in the finest sense of the term, means someone like the Robertson boys, a person who knows how to slow down, laugh at himself, get into the backwoods, live independently and recognize the value of a fellow human being.

Taking to the woods to hunt and fish, build a weekend cabin, do some trapping or simply go on a long campout doesn't leave much time for cultivating a Redneck Garden District or collecting Bibles from around the world. It's not better or worse you could say, just a different skill set. So when put side by side, which in fact they are, West Monroe and Monroe fail to meet the twin test. We can't even call them paternal twins, since it seems they were cut from two different pieces of cloth.

If not Twin Cities, perhaps a better description is Friend Cities. No one could argue with that. When our family car pulled into the PeGe parking lot in east Monroe, we felt very friendly toward our "big city" neighbors. We knew that the PeGe cooks and PeGe servers would feel friendly too when they brought us the juicy 100% beef hamburgers dripping with all the toppings. The tater tots and French fries still sizzled in their paper packages next to the burgers. The thick milk shakes, though noticeably different from Mer Rouge ice cream, washed down the thousands of delicious calories with a few hundred more. It was delicious, cheap and oh so convenient as our last stop.

After the PeGes feast we watched the sun dropping in the west, the direction of home. A bug or feeding fish made ripples here and there on the otherwise glass-like black waters of Bayou Desiard. With a very full stomach, I grew drowsy while gazing at the tall, moss-covered cypress trees growing clean out in the middle of the dark waters.

So, how do you say PeGe? Just like the letters, P and G. Next time you want a good Po'boy, hamburger or milkshake in the Friend Cities, just ask someone to point you toward the nearest respectable establishment. Likely as not you'll wind up at PeGe where the food's delicious, no matter how you say it.

"...... EVERYTHING ON THE EARTH HAS A PURPOSE, EVERY DISEASE AN HERB TO CURE IT, AND EVERY PERSON A MISSION. THIS IS THE INDIAN THEORY OF EXISTENCE."

-- MOURNING DOVE SALISH

SECRET SWAMPS

The great English missionary David Livingstone explored the continent of Africa. Jacque Cousteau plumbed the ocean deeps. Space Shuttle captain James Halsell, a West Monroe native, skimmed the edge of the earth's atmosphere. But for many West Monroe folks, the nearby dark and damp backwoods continue to entice. Anyone willing to put on heavy waders, put up with pesky biters and keep one eye always open for snakes can find in the swamps stubborn secrets more interesting than the fantasy worlds of J.RR. Tolkien or C.S. Lewis.

Sometimes the secrets come looking for you.

On a warm July day in 2008 a hotel clerk had an early start at the Ruston Fairfield Inn. The hotel sits next to I-20 at the very edge of town. Beyond it for the next 30 miles all the way to West Monroe spreads out a luxuriant and remote forest. The hilly pine country is much less fertile than the east side of the Ouachita River where huge rice and cotton crops flourish, some of which gets shipped down the Mississippi to other nations. Rust colored dirt filled with bits of low-grade iron rock covers the modest hills that rise taller the further west you go until reaching Louisiana's highest point, Driskill Mountain, topping out at a stunning 535 ft. Ruston sits on top of some decent-sized hills that serve as home to Louisiana Tech University. The top floor of Tech's Wiley Tower affords an expansive view in all directions and lets you just make out the silhouette of sturdy Driskill Mountain on the horizon.

Living with woods all around can pretty quickly make people forget they still hold many surprises. While getting her front desk tidied, the Ruston hotel clerk heard some unusual noises in the lobby. She stepped out from behind the counter for a better look...then gasped. Standing patiently at the front door, a huge black shape stared back at her. The unexpected guest peered through the glass with its beady eyes and the clerk hoped the automatic doors would stop working that morning. Unbelievably, apparently just in time for the Continental Breakfast, a 300-pound black bear had showed up on their doorstep.

The clerk rushed back to the front desk. Her shaking fingers punched in 9-1-1. We can only imagine how the transcript may have sounded:

"Police 9-1-1, can I help you?"

"Yes, I'm calling from the Fairfield Inn just off of I-20 and Highway 33."

"Yes, go ahead."

"I need to report a problem, I mean, we have an emergency. Well, it isn't exactly an emergency, not yet anyway."

"Please explain."

"I work at the front desk. Someone called me over to the front door and there was a large black bear, just outside, (*pause*) and he's still there, I can see him right now."

"A large black bear?! Did you get a good visual?"

"Yes, I'm sure, it's a bear, not a dog or anything like that. It's huge and it's looking in here right now! Can you do something, please?"

"Yes ma'am. Is he aggressive? Has it attacked anyone?"

"No, no I don't think so. It's just standing there. Maybe it's hungry. We just set out the breakfast, maybe he smelled it."

"Alright ma'am, I've dispatched the nearest squad car. Don't do anything and they'll be there in a few minutes."

"Okay, okay, I'll look for them. Thank you."

One of the employees yelled just as she hung up. "Hey, there it goes!"

The clerk rushed over to the entrance, but the bear was out of sight. Just then the police car pulled into the parking lot.

"Mornin' ma'am, we got your call," he said, his eyes narrowing. "You say there's a black bear around here?"

"Yes, I mean, it was just here, but we don't know where it went. It's couldn't have gotten far, could it? It was here just five minutes ago."

"We'll have a look, better ask everyone to stay inside until we do a survey the whole area, just in case."

The clerk turned to her co-worker and said, "I don't think he believes me, do you?"

A few minutes later the officer returned. "No sign of it ma'am, I just need you to fill out this report and then we'll get on our way."

The bear got on his way too. Maybe with hurt feelings from finding no place in the Inn, it wandered away south to the railroad tracks.

Someone just missed hitting it there and called 9-1-1 to report its location.

The police arrived at the railroad tracks where the bear escaped a near miss. Nothing. Amazed residents continued to call and report the rest of the day. "There's a bear in my back yard." "I saw a big black bear, I was afraid I might hit it." "Was that a black bear?"

By late afternoon the Wildlife and Fisheries guys showed up like calm real estate agents. They explained that the bear had probably wandered down from Arkansas and since it was comparable to a late adolescent, it was like a lot of local college students, in the mood for romance and some independent living. The bear made a logical choice for its first stop at a hotel. Where else do you stay if you're new in town? But since there were no suitable accommodations for black bears in the Ruston city limits, they would help it find more suitable real estate.

Following a couple of tips, the Wildlife officials tracked the bear down in a place you'd most likely expect to find a bear...the city park. Little Roberts Park, dubbed "Ruston's Lost Jewel," was discovered by Mr. Bear who had decided he finally had a place to get some peace and quiet. A tranquillizer gun gave him an even bigger dose of peace and quiet, enabling the officials to hoist the huge traveler into their truck for relocation in some dark forest corner where he could wander freely. For many days afterwards, jittery local residents felt some reassurance, but more often than was usual, they glanced suspiciously at the forest shadows. It would have been comforting if the Wildlife guys told exactly how far away the bear found a new home. But its whereabouts they'll never tell...it's a secret.

"THEIR FRUIT WILL
    SERVE FOR FOOD
        AND THEIR LEAVES
FOR HEALING."

-- *EZEKIEL 47:12*

HEALING LEAVES

The West Monroe school system used to resemble the way the creeks and bayous flow into one another and then all of them into the river. All the elementary schools fed a smaller number of junior high schools which in turn all fed the mammoth West Monroe High School. Eventually, no matter what part of town you came from, your social or economic class, your hobbies or accent or culture, you all wound up together in the West Monroe High School melting pot. No pun intended, though I'm sure in the old high school "smoking ring," a huge area in the middle of the campus encircled by a road, people smoked more than just cigarettes.

With sixth grade behind me at Highland, I felt a mixture of excitement and dread at the thought of moving up to Boley Junior High. It would bring together all kinds of kids from different parts of town. And though West Monroe has only 15,000 people, there are still lots of different cultures under the pines. Coming from a very conservative church-going family, I felt fear and fascination that public junior high might be just the kind of place a person could get into trouble... real fast. It didn't disappoint.

Other students in sixth grade, starting to feel the pre-teen rush of hormones, already started to show inklings of things to come. Hushed conversations on the playground and in the classroom gave rise to lots of giggling and teasing, signaling to me that something was brewing. Petty pre-teen romances between the class hotties started to come out of the shadows. Or maybe I should better say, they went into the shadows. Apparently one of the choice spots for clandestine meetings between juvenile lovers was the small patch of woods next to the neighborhood pizza joint. When I heard off-color jokes about a couple of popular classmates kissing under the trees, it colored my view of the backwoods in a whole new light. So the woods weren't just for hiking and fishing, hunting and camping anymore? The child-like, pristine, "Christopher Robin" outlook was gone, forever.

I'm amazed that any junior high teacher can succeed in implanting the smallest seed of information in the brain of their students. Hats off to junior high teachers for their patience. Some tackle the challenge and come out on top as victors, managing somehow to capture the attention and imagination of even the most foggy-headed 13-year-old. Other just give up altogether, sleeping in class behind a newspaper, waiting for the day they can draw their pension. I had some of both at Boley and both kinds elicit my respect and sympathy. I respect them all for having tried and for not simply walking out. I sympathize with them that they had to teach in a day before certain therapies and medicines have helped ease the more extreme cases of learning disorders.

Miles of woods, suburbs and town separated my home from Boley, so I had a long bus ride every morning. If a busload of halfway unhinged junior high students wasn't bad enough, our bus also delivered high school students from the same route, packing us in like crawfish in gumbo. Somewhere there must have been a regulation against three and four kids per bench. Foul language, or cussin' as we called it, fell pretty freely off the lips of school kids, but the most fluent cusser sat in complete awe of the bus driver. He could eloquently rattle off filthy, foul-mouthed, obscene strings of words in the English language in ways that hip-hop artists can only do achieve in their wildest fantasies. I never learned what he did before driving a bus. Perhaps he sailed? Worked on the ship docks? Commercial fished? Where could a person learn to cuss like that? Is there a school somewhere? Maybe at Boley Junior High? Maybe in the Smoking Circle at the high school? We couldn't drive for ten feet in any direction without a car doing something that triggered another five-minute diatribe of swearing and cursing the person, their car, their driver's license and all their progeny.

I tried to find a seat near the back. But that's where the bullies sat. I'm pretty average-sized now, but in junior high everything I ate went to my legs. So a tall, lanky, self-conscious kid sitting in the back of the bus was like duck trapped in a pen of Labrador retrievers.

Something should be clarified here. Rednecks don't exactly come in one-size-fits-all. Phil Robertson's story shows that there's rednecks of the nice sort, and then there are those that aren't. The coarse cussin' bus driver probably leaned more toward the latter. So did Phil when he ran a seedy, secluded honky-tonk somewhere near the border of Arkansas. The nicer sort of redneck still hunts and fishes and drives a pick-up truck with a gun-rack behind the driver. He may own a hunting cabin and belong to a club, chew a little tobacco and watch football on Sunday afternoon. These guys are real good neighbors and will probably give you a generous portion of venison from their recent kill. But then there's also the mean kind, and I can't really make excuses for them. I just hope things will continue to improve.

Bullies in any shape or form can make life pretty miserable for the underdog. The redneck bullies made me wish I could avoid the bus altogether by getting to school the old-fashioned way of walking leisurely on a trail through the woods. That not an option, I hunkered down every day and tried to find a seat about half-way back in a sort of Mason-Dixon line where I couldn't hear the bus driver's ungodly orations and didn't have some pushy upperclassman trying to steal my bag.

With the abundance of squirrel-shooting, pickup-driving good-ole-boys streaming into the local school system every day, most of whom only consented to the whole public school educational experiment because of all the dainty (and not so dainty) Southern gals also being herded into the same situation, someone in the administration came up with a brilliant idea of including hunter safety in the health class. That went pretty well, with Coach, a short man with a very red face, giving lessons each day on how to safely transport a rifle or shotgun, what kind of clothing to wear to avoid being accidentally shot and how to get help in the event of emergency. The course culminated with a field trip outside of West Monroe to heavily wooded grounds where all the students got try a few shots on the skeet range. Some of the boys, who had started hunting around 2 of age, could fling up the 12-gauge like a whip when Coach shouted out,

"PULL!" Never missing, these true woodsmen shamed some of us softer suburban types.

Daddy did not much enjoy hunting or fishing, so up to then my only exposure to guns came at Pawpaw's farm, where he kept them on hand to scare off coyotes or shoot a pesky rat or chicken snake. When my turn came to shoot skeet, I lugged up the heavy 12-gauge and waited nervously for Coach to shout. When the mighty "PULL" echoed off the nearby trees, I pulled the trigger, aiming rather wildly for the little Frisbee-shaped clay skeet. I had three chances, and I remember-- or at least prefer to remember-- that I nicked the last one, saving me from complete disgrace. It wasn't a day to establish myself as a redneck among rednecks.

At the end of 8th grade, the cruel joke was that instead of showing one of the boys who could handle a shotgun with Olympic style grace and skill, the school yearbook contained a photo of me in huge bell-bottom jeans, desperately trying to hold the shotgun level with the ground while not suddenly tumbling over backwards. It might have been a piece of planned propaganda to subtly convey the message, "anyone can be a redneck, or at least fall over trying."

In later years my physical coordination caught up with my lanky limbs and I enjoyed many good hunting trips with friends. But for me the woods were first and always primarily a place for peaceful solitude, a place for healing. After exhausting days of dealing with tired-out teachers, lengthy lessons, bored bullies and desperate teen-age dramas, I stepped off the school bus in front of our home, tossed my book bag aside, grabbed my walking stick and escaped into the woods. The noisy kids on the bus slowly faded as it chugged away down the road to its next stop and the sounds of chattering blue-jays and an occasional wood-pecker high in the tree-tops took their place.

By this time in life my excursions took me far beyond the barb-wire fence where Daddy took us years earlier. I discovered a large terrain that supported some of the finest variety of trees, swamps, hills, lowlands and uplands anywhere around. Wondering exactly where the creek flowed after it went through our back yard, I followed foot by foot along its twisting and winding way, until I eventually came to the end of the lengthy wetlands quite some distance from our home but much closer to the West Monroe city limits. Amazingly, this pristine Louisiana wilderness, which was much bigger then but still partly remains untouched, survived the slow encroachment of humans. Gigantic pen oaks, sweet gum, cypress and hickory grew in the rich black dirt of the bottoms, nourished by countless floods in the wide flat spaces around the creek. Rising up abruptly from the flat bottoms, 100-foot hills supported large stands of tall pines. The verdant pine groves covered the forest floor with tons of soft, reddish pine straw. The soft carpet helped keep down the annoying briars and underbrush and created a peaceful and quiet environment where man and beast could walk soundlessly.

Two of the best trees that could be found scattered here and there along the edges of the swamp were the holly and the cedar. Holly trees never lose their glossy green leaves and produce beautiful red berries. Somehow they had a clean and wholesome feeling; maybe that's why they show up in so many Christmas decorations. The Louisiana cedar (really a member of the juniper family) is also an evergreen, so it stands out warmly in the dense winter forest when everything else along the creeks and on the hills has turned a dull gray. With heavy needles on its upper branches, the cedar's lower branches slowly wither and die, leaving the old growth sticking out near the bottom like brittle old bones. In someone's yard this old growth is usually pruned off. In the woods however where it remains unpruned, this old growth has a special property that keeps it from rotting. Cedar heartwood is a brilliantly rich shade of purplish-red, is durable and has the added feature of a pleasant aroma. The nature of cedar wood makes it rot-resistant, so an old cedar tree is a treasure chest…as furniture-makers know and Phil Robertson proved with his famous duck calls.

The world behind me and the forest before me, I walked carelessly under the oak and pine canopies, my eye always open for both friendly critters and those not so friendly. The cares and worries of belligerent bus drivers, rude rednecks and just being a teen-ager went away like a dry shell falling off a locust.

To be honest, I also felt the presence of the Lord. Time alone in the West Monroe backwoods wasn't a replacement for being with people, it was replenishment so I could be with people, so I could understand them and forgive them. I thought about that when I visited a particular old tree near the barb-wire fence. Over the years its bark relentlessly grew around and concealed the barb-wire. The tree had suffered, yet had overcome. The healing leaves quietly reminded me that discomfort, pain or even death are not final. The sap will rise again in the sweet gum. The fragrant heartwood will develop in the cedar. The oak will reach higher and higher for the sky. Life will come. Life is final.

"SAFE?" SAID MR. BEAVER; "DON'T YOU
HEAR WHAT MRS. BEAVER TELLS YOU?
WHO SAID ANYTHING ABOUT SAFE?
'COURSE HE ISN'T SAFE. BUT HE'S GOOD.
HE'S THE KING, I TELL YOU."

— *C.S. LEWIS, THE LION, THE WITCH, AND THE
WARDROBE*

CHRISTMAS BOOTS AND BEAVERS

Santa Claus may tromp around in the Artic snow and ice warmed by his shiny black boots, but one Christmas my folks presented me a most amazing backwoods gift that rivaled anything of his.

From its very beginning as a hunting camp, West Monroe was a rowdy and rough place. Frontiersmen, hunters, trappers, traders and rabble-rousers loitered and lazed under the shady trees right along with the mosquitoes and raccoons. Little by little civic-minded settlers moved in and created a friendly and prosperous— if not still a little rowdy—river port on the Ouachita. The big cash crop was cotton. So before it was called West Monroe, the town was named Cottonport. Old steamboats loaded up at Cottonport and chugged away down the river with cotton bales piled high as smoke-stacks. Not wasting any part of the cotton plant, Cottonport built the Union Cottonseed Oil Mill. It looked right out over the river and gave good jobs to lots of new settlers.

Cottonport's downtown section grew up around the river docks and cottonseed mill with fresh buildings for storage, mercantile and clerical activity. When the townsfolk applied for a new post office, they had to find a new town name, since there was already another Cottonport. They decided on West Monroe and continued to develop their new settlement with more streets and homes and businesses.

With gradual changes in the Old South, the river was used less and less for shipping cotton, the oil mill's business slacked off and the tidy little shops and offices along West Monroe's riverfront feel into disuse. Signs started to sag, paint started to peel and long lonely sidewalks running from the cottonseed mill toward the rail track became a depressing stroll that no one bothered to take anymore. In the 1990's this completely changed with the downtown revitalization of Antique Ally. But during my youth, we watched as one by one, most of the town's old businesses closed their shutters for good or move out to the interchange on I-20.

Things downtown got worse when the giant cottonseed elevator at Union Mill caught fire. Instead of going up in a huge blaze of flames, one of the big round silos settled into a slow smolder after firefighters doused it in water. Smoke from downtown billowed up over West Monroe like a cloud, covering the town with a stomach-turning stench of damp and smoldering cotton seed. It smelled like rotting cheese, but no one could escape it, at least not without just turning the other direction and running as far as you could. West Monroe already had an odor problem because of the paper mill pumping waste products into the air and swamps. On a bad day, when the clouds hung low and the humidity shot up high, the air over West Monroe had a unique aroma. Some said it stank, others said it was the smell of money. The pile of rotting and burning cotton seed next to the Ouachita combining with the paper mill's special gift made it seem like no one in West Monroe ever took a bath, which probably confirmed what the Monroe people already suspected.

A few die-hards near ole' Cottonport refused to leave downtown, in spite of the foul odors, the dilapidated warehouses and the sagging oak trees lining the riverfront. When everyone else seemed to be fleeing for high ground in the new suburbs popping up to the west and north, First Baptist Church kept its property just a few blocks away from the river and the old West Monroe High School. A jeweler or two continued selling trinkets and watches on Trenton Street just down from the cotton seed mess. A local hardware store across from Union Mill tenaciously held on, though the owner lived outside of town just down the street from our home in the woods.

Then one year, something remarkable happened.

I never learned who had the vision to undertake something so innovative in a declining 1980s Southern town, but someone rented an old house behind First Baptist and converted it into an all-round adventure sports center and called it simply, Outdoor Adventures. Like something out of my dreams, Outdoor Adventures had a rustic brown exterior, natural wood floors and warmly lighted rooms crammed floor to ceiling with all kinds of backpacks, freeze-dried foods, canoes, kayaks, sweaters, rain and snow gear, cook stoves, maps, snake-bite kits, hats, scarves, helmets, survival books, tents, ropes, straps, connectors, compasses, binoculars, socks, walking sticks, sleeping bags, parkas, bug-repellent and my personal favorite, hand-crafted leather hiking boots imported from the Italian Alps. In that very first visit to Outdoor Adventures my hope and faith in mankind revived.

One of my driving goals after graduating high school was to hike a portion of the Appalachian Trail. Outdoor Adventures' arrival in West Monroe with their incredible selection of gear and experienced staff made my dream of pushing out my horizon to the great Appalachian backcountry suddenly become much more realistic. I had trekked through the Tupawek backwaters countless times by my senior year and wanted more challenges.

Acquiring a US Geological Survey topo map of west Ouachita parish, I discovered that the hill country to our north rose higher and then suddenly dropped steeply into thousands of acres of swampy wilderness designated as the D'Arbonne National Wildlife Refuge. Years earlier Daddy took me into this low country searching for huckleberry thickets where we would fill our buckets, eager to see the delicious berries make a fat cobbler that evening. Back then I didn't know much else about the D'Arbonne refuge except that just past the West Monroe city limits the highway dropped into a shady low land, occupied by only a few folks living in houses built on stilts. Past the stilt-houses the road ran straight as an arrow for miles, flanked by foreboding trees that sported long beards of gray moss. The USGS map lifted some of the mystery and showed me new trails to follow in search of more backwoods unspoiled by houses and stores. Taking multiple hikes through the D'Arbonne refuge and then later reading Peter Jenkins' trekking story in *A Walk Across America* fueled my desire for a major-league backwoods rite of passage.

After church and school, Outdoor Adventures became a base

of regular operations. A good family friend named Carl mentored me in the finer aspects of backpacking and hiking gear, setting me on the right track from the very beginning. I learned the difference between an external frame and internal frame backpack, the importance of having good maps, how to improve the taste of freeze-dried food (actually not possible to do), and what kind of inclement weather emergencies to prepare for when hitting the deep backcountry. Outdoor Adventures staff pitched in with good advice now and again, but not with quite the same unbiased objectivity as Carl. Fair enough, they wanted to sell merchandise. On the other hand, I wanted quality, for a bargain.

My parents, particularly Momma, expressed hesitation about my bold idea to spend three months on the Appalachian Trail. She had read somewhere that a couple of hikers had been shot to death on the trail. Okay, I said, that's too bad; but it's not like a war zone or anything. Then again, there was the bear problem, especially along the 100 miles section through the Great Smokey Mountain Park. True too, but the bears almost never eat anything different from the average Sunday football couch potato…Coke and chips. Three months is a long time. I had to agree on that point, and in order to secure a hiking partner, we whittled down the hike to five days in June in the Great Smokey Mountain Park.

With the place and date picked, I studied the equipment at Outdoor Adventures even more carefully. On the very back wall of the showroom, standing on a series of small perches, various Italian hiking boots looked as though they were in the very act of scaling the Matterhorn. I gingerly removed one from its mountain goat ledge and examined every stitch and knot. It had bright red boot laces that could have held the weight of a grown man in the event one of the climbing ropes broke. The soles had layers of real leather pressed together on top of heavy, black tread. Knobby grips provided necessary traction for any terrain. The top was a tough brown leather unlike anything I had seen. There were two leather tongues in the boot, one fitting snuggly on the foot and the outer one repelling all kinds of snow or ice, mud or water.

One problem. I didn't have any money, certainly not the $110 that the boots cost. These days that works out to almost $300. I had a part-time job vacuuming and emptying the trash bins at the new McMillan Mall near I-20, but even so the purchase was beyond my means. I had studied and read and hiked in all kinds of second-hand waders and steel-toed factory boots and I knew, I mean I KNEW, that those sturdy Italian boots and only those boots could reliably carry me into the backcountry.

December came around, bringing the typical wet, not white, Christmas. The day of Christmas toys stuffed into stockings passed me by years earlier. Even the prospect of a graduation trip to hike the Appalachian Trail couldn't fully lift my spirits that Christmas. I was still nursing the wounds of a failed romance. West Monroe High had plenty of guys already shaving daily to stem the growth of a redneck beard and no short supply of mostly grown-up girls eager to be noticed. It produced an atmosphere charged with fumes…perfumes and auto fumes, as the chase was on. When it came to facial hair, I remember having a stray whisker sprout out one time on my neck just next to my none too subtle Adam's apple. As for car fumes, driving down Cypress Street in Momma's old Chevrolet Impala may have turned heads, but not for the right reasons. Past the age of sugar plums and elves and down on my luck with the ladies, I went into the Christmas holiday just sort of hoping it would pass quickly.

Right up to Christmas Eve Momma was still expressing misgivings about the Appalachian adventure. I tried to not let it bother me too much while we swapped gifts that evening. Piles of festively wrapped presents flowed from under the tree. As was our custom we gathered together in the family room after supper for the Nativity reading that always preceded the gift opening. In a melancholy mood I listened to the familiar tale of the star, the village, the animals and Joseph and Mary's trek through the Judean backcountry. I couldn't deny that everything was beautiful. Gathered as a family next to the fireplace, we enjoyed the simple and familiar trappings of Christmas. The red bows, green wreaths, collectible ornaments and Christmas carols softly playing on the stereo set the stage for Daddy's gentle voice. "And it came to pass in those days…" Waiting much more patiently than we did ten years earlier, my sisters and I listened thoughtfully until he finished.

Momma got up and started sifting through the gifts. Carrie excitedly added her instructions and pointed under the tree. The Bible reading completed, we suddenly found ourselves feeling more like children than anyone cared to admit. Presents went out in every direction. I opened a couple of packages before Momma handed me an envelope. A Christmas card? It felt anti-climactic. I popped it open. A note fluttered down.

I looked at it and gasped. "Good for one pair of hiking boots," it said in Momma's hand-writing. This was it! I thanked my folks and tried my best to keep my cool demeanor, but inside I wanted to burst. Alpine boots, you would be mine.

The first opening day after Christmas, I drove downtown to Outdoor Adventures armed with a signed check from my folks. I parked outside the rustic shop and dashed inside. Knowing exactly which pair I hoped to buy, I quickly tried on the boots. Perfect boots, perfect size. Cinderella's glass slippers didn't fit any better (and probably cost less). The salesman carefully placed the new boots into a sturdy cardboard box cleverly designed to look like planks of wood. The rich smell of several different kinds of tanned leather filled the air, driving out any memory of smoldering cotton seed or paper mill waste.

Months earlier my brother-in-law Mike, a trained naturalist from Shreveport, introduced me to a substantially large beaver lodge and dam built on the edge of town where a large creek fed into the Ouachita River. The Christmas school break gave me time to lace up my new boots for a "maiden trek" into the local goo. I suspect the Italian boot maker lovingly cut his seasoned leather and stitched each tiny loop with expectations that a brawny Swiss mountaineer would use the boots to scale a craggy pass in the Old Country. But I donned boots and thought, "Yeah, whatever!" These boots had forsaken the Old Country and the snowy mountains. Just a few feet above sea level in Louisiana, *nouveau* territory awaited.

Driving my way up North 7th, wearing my boots freshly waterproofed with bees wax from Outdoor Adventures, I looked for the turnoff into the riverside woodlands. It didn't take too long to get to the dirt lane that took me away from a few houses and trailers and along a barb-wire fence marking someone's pasture. Past the pasture the trees grew thicker and the ground wetter. It flattened out and the soil was bare due to the constant washing of the floodwaters.

I found a good place to park on a dry spot. Sunlight filtered through the treetops, but the temperature dropped to nearly freezing, making for a brisk December day. I left the car behind and started hiking down the dirt road. The semi-wilderness called to mind Narnia's Aslan; like the great lion it was good, but not necessarily safe.

The occasional mudhole enticed me. These boots were designed for extremities. I splashed down in the water and mud, seizing the moment to feel invincible with my new boots. Hiking onward I came to the end of the lane. It stopped abruptly next to a large pool. The swirling of the river backwaters and the busy activity of the beavers under the low cypress branches created a perfect Louisiana lagoon. Just a little beyond the beaver dam, a large creek flowed lazily into the river. My new boots had brought me to an old friend. They brought me to the mouth of Tupawek Bayou.

The beavers must have been busy with their own Christmas celebrations, because they never peeped out, even for a brief holiday greeting. I tromped around for an hour or two beside the water taking in the brisk air, the sounds of water fowl and the constantly changing ripples in the river's current. The water flowed and flowed, never stopping, never returning. The beavers lived in a piece of prime real estate. Clever beasts.

After sticky goo put two pounds on my new boots, I scraped off as much as I could with a stick. The western sky became a hue of deep blue lined by gold. The silhouettes of tall pines in the distance grew black.

Time to leave.

I hesitated to rush away from such a perfect moment. I had my new boots, the hiding beavers were my only company and the crisp evening air put a healthy jolt in my lungs. I watched the river currents lazily flowing past one last time. I knew that's how things go. I couldn't stay there forever. After a last deep breath I got in the car. Cherish the moment…carry on with the current…clean the mud off your boots.

"I NEVER SAW A MAN WITH HIS FACE SHAVED CLEAN UNTIL I WAS A BIG BOY. WHEN I SAW HIM I THOUGHT HE WAS A DEAD MAN...WALKING ABOUT, AND I WAS MIGHTY SCARED."

-- BEN LILLY, BACKWOODSMAN

FARTHER INTO THE BACKWOODS

Winter at Pawpaw and Mawmaw's brought gray skies that deluged the empty cotton fields around their farm. Snow rarely fell and the continual rain turned thousands of square miles of countryside into a slick layer of world-class Louisiana gloop. Our car couldn't reach the farm except by driving down several miles of unpaved road. Once or twice during the summer the parish maintenance department managed to rustle up an antique road grader and send it scraping down the one-lane track. If they had a little extra money in the budget they might drop a fresh layer of gravel. It worked fine when the hot summer sun baked the road as hard as granite. Those days were quickly forgotten with the onslaught of winter mud.

Water standing in the fields, mud six inches deep on the road and a steady drizzle of cold rain discouraged any serious attempt to explore the outdoors. During those times, the best place to pass the time was a comfortable seat next to the little butane heater warming the farmhouse living room. A hundred tiny blue flames burned happily in the heater, generating enough heat to drive out all thoughts of muddy boots and soaking jeans.

Pawpaw had a deer-hide rocking chair where he could sit right up close to the heater, warm his feet and "visit." Visiting among the local folks could mean a number of things, but it was bound to include a few good stories. One of my favorite treats at Mawmaw and Pawpaw's wasn't the hot rolls with hand-churned butter but finding Pawpaw in a relaxed mood where he could just sit and recollect some of his childhood days in the backwoods.

"Pawpaw, can you tell me about Ben Lilly?" I knew just how to prime the pump. His face lighted up and a story quickly followed.

"Ben Lilly, yes, he was a great hunter, spent time around these parts, traveling up and down the Mississippi river. He used to stop in here and visit with my folks. They'd feed him a hot meal and have a good visit."

I could sense adventure afoot in the house. "What did he hunt?" I asked, already knowing the answers to the questions since I'd asked them a hundred times before.

"What'd he hunt? Why, he could hunt anything. He killed black bears and panthers, just about anything there was. They say one time he had to shoot his own horse."

"His own horse, why's that?"

"Well, you see, he had been out huntin' all day for black bears. He was a good hunter and had killed an awful lot of bears so he finally shot one that day. He had his horse along with him and he wanted to put the bear on the horse to carry it back to his camp. Now that horse wasn't interested in havin' a dead bear throwed up on his back and so he went to buckin' and pawin' like he was just gonna' kill Ben Lilly right there in the woods."

"That's terrible," I uttered, expressing my sincere interest.

"I suppose it was. When the horse reared up he knocked Ben Lilly over and was just about to step on him. His rifle got knocked out his hands and he had to grab it quick. So that's when he had to shoot the animal to keep from havin' it step on him."

"What would make the horse do that?" I said, eager for more.

"Horses are skittish creatures sometimes and if they get spooked, they can rear up. I reckon that one just didn't like the bear and shore didn't want to be carryin' it around on its back."

"Then what happened?"

"With a dead bear and a dead horse, I reckon Ben must have had to carry that o' bear by himself."

This was always a good transition to ask about Pawpaw's own backwoods adventures. "Did you ever hunt a bear?"

"No, not really. Weren't many left around here when I was a little feller."

"But you did ride a horse in the woods, didn't you?"

He chuckled and said, "You had to ride a horse, that was the only way we could bring in the hogs. They didn't stay in the pasture, we'd turn 'em loose in the woods. They'd feed all summer and we'd have to go round 'em up."

I had seen *Old Yeller*, so this modern kid knew something at least about rounding up feral hogs. "That was dangerous, wasn't it?" I asked, eager for the dramatic details.

"Yes, sometimes a mean ole' hog with long tusks would just tear open the side of a dog."

"They were mean!"

"That's just their nature to protect their little ones. We would bring the dog home with a bandage and the women folk would sew him up."

"You mean it lived?"

"I've seen a dog with his innards showing get sowed up and get back out in the woods to chase more hogs."

The backwoods remedies intrigued me. "Did you have medicine?" I asked.

Pawpaw rocked back and forth and answered, "Just a little coal oil on the wound."

After my first scraps and scratches on the farm I learned quickly that Pawpaw's cure-all was coal oil. Momma said she once saw him cut his leg to the bone, then douse it with coal oil and wrap it tightly with a bandage. After a week or two the leg emerged like new. "Did the hogs ever attack you?"

"You had to be real careful, watch your legs and keep a tree or the horse or something else always between you and them. They could turn on you real fast."

As he talked I tried to imagine the forest before the logging and farming had all but razed it. Pawpaw said that when he was young a person could travel for thirty miles in dense bottomland from Oak Grove to Bastrop. Today the land supports a multimillion dollar rice industry that supplies nations as far away as China. Yet I couldn't help but wonder what kind of life those dark swamps must have harbored before the arrival of loggers and farmers.

"Tell me about fishing on the Boeuf River," I said, changing the subject to one of Pawpaw's favorites. "Didn't you say that people used to catch catfish with their bare hands?"

"Oh yes, catfish, bullfrogs, and sometimes snakes," he said with a glint in his bright eyes. "Before they cleared out the Boeuf River it was full of logs and stumps and the catfish loved hidin' down in those places. And all along the riverbank the frogs would hide out in holes. When I was a boy we'd go down along the river when the water was low and reach up into them holes. You could feel along for a fat bullfrog leg and just pull him out."

Warming my own hands close to the glowing heater I asked, "Did you catch any?"

"Yeah, but one time I put my hand deep into a hole and felt around. Something was in there and it felt like a big fat frog leg. I grabbed ahold and pulled it out."

My ears perked up with excitement. "What happened then?"

"It wasn't a big frog after all. I had grabbed a cotton mouth by mistake!"

Thankfully Pawpaw quickly tossed it aside before the ornery

viper could figure out what happened to disturb its naptime; otherwise I might not have come along to hear about its exciting day on the riverside.

I eagerly asked for more stories. "Can you tell me about catching catfish in the logs?"

Pawpaw rocked some more, happy to oblige. "In those days the Boeuf was full of stumps and logs and it made a good place for the catfish. I reckon some of them went in those hollowed out places where they had a nest. Folks round here figured out you could feel along the shallow places in the hollow logs and find where the big catfish were hiding. I remember one time a couple of fellers were down on the Boeuf and found a great big catfish in one of them logs. It was so big they couldn't pull it out, so they got a rope tied up round its head and tied the other end to their horse."

"That's unbelievable! How big were those fish?"

"Oh my Sugar, some of them fish were bigger than you."

"Did they ever get it out?"

"Yeah, I believe so. One of them stayed down in the water with his foot in the front of the log so the fish couldn't get away until they got that rope on it. Then that horse gave a good pull and they got it up. I'm sure it weighed a lot."

"You caught some big ones too, didn't you?" I asked, feeling quite sorry by then that the Corps of Engineers had ever bothered to practically sterilize the sluggish backwaters of the Boeuf.

"Oh yes, we fished down there all the time. One time my

father and I set out some lines along riverside and the next morning we went back to check 'em. I remember one of the lines was hanging there in the water from a branch and it wasn't moving or anything, so I told my father nothing was there. We started pulling it up to put some more bait on it when I noticed that it was awful heavy."

"So you did have something."

"Yep, I pulled and pulled and there was a great big old catfish, maybe twenty or thirty pounds."

To provide Mawmaw a convenient place to satisfy her love for fishing and to give his grandkids a taste of his own childhood adventures, Pawpaw built a big fish pond in the middle of his pasture and stocked it with catfish. He fed them every day so they fattened up like their wild cousins in the nearby rivers and bayous. Among our extended family a myth developed that said there was a monster catfish submerged in the pond's deepest hole. With every five or six pound catfish we caught out of the pond, the monster fish myth grew larger and larger. We became convinced that it was in the little farm pond, smirking at us like the elusive Loch Ness Monster, eating all the little fish and stealing food from the big ones. When something occasionally broke our fish line or pulled huge chunks of bait off a set-hook, it confirmed our suspicions and we tried to imagine how big the creature would get before the only thing that could stop its growth was the size of the pond.

After respiratory problems took Mawmaw early, Pawpaw stayed on the home place for many more years. Daddy called him a tough old boot when he decided in his seventies to build a new barn. Fiercely loyal, he never showed any interest in remarrying and lived to 94, contenting himself with visits from his children, grandchildren and great-grandchildren. His sharp wit and excellent memory often carried many of us deep into the backwoods, if we would only take the time to sit at his feet and listen.

"I'M ALWAYS INTERESTED IN LOOKING
FORWARD TOWARD THE FUTURE.
CARVING OUT NEW WAYS OF LOOKING AT
THINGS."

-- HERBIE HANCOCK

WHITTLIN'

One summer I traded the Tupawek for the Kisatchie National Forest, packing into a rickety school-bus-become-church-bus for a week of summer camp. My first week away from home came when I was about 9 and I wasn't any too sure about the experience. Old Highway 165 between Monroe and Alexandria was somewhat better than a logging trail, but the bus trip to church camp still took us a couple of hours through the dense pine forest in the central Louisiana highlands. Each summer until my late teens I repeated the trip, having developed close friendships and learning to deeply appreciate both the natural and spiritual environment deep in the Kisatchie woodlands.

The small town of Olla came half-way to camp and if the driver timed it just right we reached the Olla Dairy Queen for lunch. Forget all the TV celeb chefs and drop the big-city cookeries. Hands down, those little Southern ladies running the Olla Dairy Queen could fix some of the best hamburgers in the world served next to the creamiest milk-shakes and crispiest tater-tots.   When you live hundreds of miles from a big city, surrounded by nothing but dense pine forest in a town with hungry truckers and loggers, you have time to bring these simple pleasures of life as near to perfection as is humanly possible. For some mysterious reason in the divine plan, our bus load of hungry campers, going to and returning from a week in the woods, were among the chosen who could savor the feast not just once but twice each year.

With happily satisfied stomachs, our bus arrived at Camp Pollack an hour later filled with that unique mixture of emotions that only summer camp can illicit. Would we make a new friend, did a new romance await us, was the speaker boring or inspiring, would someone raid our cabin with shaving cream and toilet paper? The possibilities excited and frightened.

Joining a dozen other nervous boys at the rugged cabin I tossed my bags and bedding onto a reclaimed army bunk. Screens surrounded us, keeping out the mosquitoes but letting in the slightest cricket's chirp and snap of a twig. We had no electronics, the bathhouse was a five-minute walk with no guarantee of hot water and the mess hall looked no different from our rustic cabin except only bigger.

After only a year or two of attending camp, I fell in love with the open-air cabins, the gravel roads, the deep woods and most of all, the delightful characters who volunteered each summer to serve us kids. One of them was the camp night watchman, a little man with gray hair whom we called Brother Norvell. Somehow he brought to mind one of the woodland dwarves in the story of *Snow White*, but one with thick glasses and no beard. He usually wore a loose-fitting pair of blue-jean overalls softened by countless washings. It always had a smooth piece of cedar sticking out the top pocket.

Each evening when the sun fell out of sight giving relief from the intense heat, Brother Norvell started stirring about with the other forest creatures. Camp Pollack covered several dozen acres next to Highway 165 on the border of Kisatchie National Park. His job, though not particularly dangerous, took him along all the dirt roads and trails of the sprawling camp where he could keep an eye open for a stray boy planning a clandestine meeting with a girl or a skunk who might have wandered under a cabin. All night long little Brother Norvell stealthily padded around under the camp pines. We never knew when or where he would suddenly turn up. If one of the boys' cabins got a little rowdy after lights out, Brother Norvell would suddenly emerge from the inky darkness and frighten us to sleep with a gentle but firm reprimand.

One of my good camp friends, a strapping country boy named Van from the Bonadee swamps near Bonita, got me interested in what every Southern boy must learn to use at a young age...pocketknives. Mawmaw, eager to move me along toward proper manhood, gave me a solid little black pocketknife for Christmas one year. Later at summer camp, Van and I became devoted fans of Brother Norvell, the master whittler.

Night watching at a sleepy little summer camp left plenty of time for Brother Norvell to refine his carving skills. Every hour or so he'd make his rounds and once he felt satisfied that everything was in place, he'd find a comfortable stump or railroad tie to sit down and whittle. We learned to follow his trail by looking for piles of cedar shavings in a variety of places like the spacious fire circle, the wooden bench on the mess hall porch and an old log close to the swimming pool. By following cedar shavings the next morning we could retrace his trail from the previous night. We wouldn't see him moving around camp until dusk that evening. Rested from his good day's sleep, he was happy to sit with his enthralled disciples and let us watch his whizzing pocketknife cut the red, aromatic wood, making the shavings pile higher and higher. His calloused hands may have been nicked on occasion by the razor-sharp blade, but it only made them tougher. I could never get my knife blade as sharp as his nor could I get my piece of cedar nearly as smooth. He whittled and cut until the red heartwood became smooth as a polished piece of fine marble. With backwoods precision he wielded a knife to make a piece of sculpture from a scraggly cedar branch.

Each summer while on his night rounds, Brother Norvell whittled down his store of cedar to pass the time. He wasn't aiming to create fine art or even something practical. I suppose, though I never asked, that he prayed for all of us while he walked and whittled. He just seemed like that kind of man; like someone who saved up his words for talking with God under the starry skies of Kisatchie.

Like good disciples, we took Brother Norvell's lessons to heart. I put together a collection of pocketknives and hunting knives. The most important tool I ever learned to keep with me at all times was the Swiss Army Knife. While traveling in remote places like the steppes of Kazakhstan, the rocky beaches of Cyprus and the mountains of Turkey, I've used my pocketknife countless times to rescue myself from a potentially disastrous mechanical breakdown. In his adult years, my buddy Van took his interest in knife-craft to a new level. He built a blacksmith shop and learned how to forge blades of exceptional strength. His knives fetched a good price and earned him a wide reputation for quality craftsmanship. For a while he lived in Central America, assisting the local churches build their own forges for knife-making and other useful blacksmithing. I don't know if Brother Norvell ever learned about Van's adventures or mine. But if he ever did hear how we profited from observing his simple lifestyle of sittin' and whittlin', I know he would give us one great big smile from behind his thick glasses.

"AND I WILL PUT ENMITY BETWEEN YOU AND THE WOMAN, AND BETWEEN YOUR OFFSPRING AND HERS; HE WILL CRUSH YOUR HEAD, AND YOU WILL STRIKE HIS HEEL"

-- *Genesis 3:15*

SNAKE BITE

While we're on the subject of Camp Pollack, I might as well tell about the time a pigmy rattlesnake bit my sister Carrie. The Louisiana woodlands and swamps have no end of snakes. Being coldblooded, snakes don't do so well the farther north you go, although I should mention that I've been very surprised over the years to discover that the water moccasin can be found as far north as Indiana. Some of those rascally critters have an amazing ability to get far enough underground to avoid a deep freeze. But nowhere is quite as snake-friendly as the Gulf Coast. The poisonous crawlers include the cottonmouth, timber rattler, pigmy rattler, coral snake and copperhead. Given the number and distribution of poisonous reptiles, one could reasonably expect a large number of snakebites every year. But except on rare occasions, people and snakes manage to give each other a wide berth. Carrie was one of those rare occasions.

Being several years older than me, my sisters attended camp different weeks than I. They enjoyed it for many of the same reasons I did, like seeing best friends and getting into a natural environment. Carrie packed a big suitcase with her things and took off for camp, eager to see her best friend Pam. The girls stayed in the same kind of open-air cabins the boys did and they had to walk several minutes down to the gray cinder-block bathhouses. Unlike the boys, especially the boys under 13, the girls usually spent lots more time in the bathhouses primping in front of the mirrors until late at night.

The bathhouse was not only an important place for primping and grooming, it was a noisy center of social life. Girls came and went from the nearest bathhouses, trying to carefully step over the pools of shower water splashed onto the cement floor and into the footpath leading back to the cabins. A couple of small outdoor lights cast a pale glow on the footpath, yielding just enough light for someone to see the outline of the pathway. Most kids brought flashlights to camp so they could safely navigate the distance between the cabins and the bathhouses. But even a flashlight could only help so much and just beyond its reach the pitch black of the forest engulfed everyone.

After the worship meeting one evening, Carrie and her friends headed back to their cabin feeling sleepy and ready for bed. They got their toiletries and walked down to the nearest bathhouse as was their routine. The bare light bulbs in the bathhouse guided them down the hill. They laughed and talked, enjoying the peaceful evening. Carrie finished brushing her teeth, got her things and started back to the cabin. She stepped into the damp footpath and walked a few steps when suddenly she felt a sharp sting on her left ankle. She cried out in pain and surprise. The other girls wanted to know what was going on, but Carrie didn't know exactly what to say. They examined the pebbly pathway for any sign of something unusual, but it was all guesswork. Maybe she had stepped on a thorn or brushed against an ant hill. As they walked back to the cabin the small group of girls talked and started to consider a frightening possibility...did a snake bite Carrie?

Each cabin had at least one adult counselor. The woods surrounding Camp Pollack may have been crawling with snakes, but rarely did the counselors ever have to see one of them pop up inside the camp. When the girls brought Carrie to the cabin, the counselor listened to their story. Nothing to do but carefully examine her ankle. They shined as much light onto the ankle as they could muster with their generous supply of flashlights. The counselor looked closely while the area rapidly swelled. The examination confirmed their worst fears. Just below the ankle bone they could clearly see two red holes, just the size and shape they would expect from the needle-like fangs of a poisonous snake.

Making haste, the camp leaders got Carrie into a car and drove her to the nearest hospital some miles away. Girls in pajamas somberly stood to the side while the adults gathered some of her things and loaded the car. There was no time to waste. No one knew for sure what kind of snake had bitten her ankle. The two small holes were less than a centimeter apart; they hoped that meant the snake could deliver only a small amount of venom. But the foot continued to grow bigger and she was obviously in pain.

The car sped down the highway with a scared and suffering Carrie. Her kind friends did their best to comfort and reassure her that it wasn't her fault to get a snake bite by simply going to the bathhouse. At the hospital they quickly moved her into the emergency room. The medical staff looked at her ankle under the bright lights. A quick assessment of her blood pressure and heart rate confirmed the presence of a powerful poison in her system. If a person had to get a snake bite, the ankle was one of the safest places because of its thin skin and distance from the heart. With a grave look on his face, the doctor looked up from the ankle and instructed the nurse to get a certain vial of antivenin. They cleaned the punctures and administered some other medication to relieve her pain. He explained to the camp staff that he thought it most likely Carrie disturbed a little pygmy rattler on the trail. They are very well camouflaged and can be hard to see even in the full daylight. To make matters worse, pygmy rattlers have a nasty disposition. They may only grow to one or two feet in length, but carry themselves like a 12-foot giant. Their bite is one of the most common in the Deep South. It usually isn't fatal for a healthy adult, but can cause tremendous pain, swelling and open blisters.

The nurse returned and injected Carrie with a dose of antivenin, then relocated her to a hospital room. The camp director called our parents with the news that she would have to stay in the hospital for a couple of days so they could continue treatment and keep an eye on her for any complications. Momma and Daddy threw some of their things in a bag and took off to be with Carrie.

For a tense few days Carrie lay in the hospital slowly regaining her strength. The snake venom spread across her foot and up to her knee. When she came home with our folks, we waited anxiously at the door to see just how bad things had been. Momma helped her walk from the car to the house. She hobbled with difficulty, unable to put any weight on the left foot. My eyes widened when I got my first look at her leg. That little creepy snake shot enough venom in her to turn her foot and leg completely black, like one gigantic bruise. Furthermore, it made her leg swell to a least twice its regular size.

For a few days at least Carrie and I called a truce in our on-going arguing and pestering. We all did what we could to make her more comfortable and slowly recuperate from the rattlesnake bite. I gained a rather profound new sense of respect for the power of nature. The next time I took a stroll in the forest I kept an extra eye open for the tell-tale signs of a snake slithering through the leaves strewn over the forest floor. Never fond of snakes, I became less of a fan. I knew that little belly-crawler didn't bite my sister out of malice, but the realization hardly diminished the coldness in my heart to anything with a diamond shaped head and fangs. On several occasions in subsequent years I found myself face-to-fang with poisonous snakes which either crawled up into our backyard or barred my way on a forest trail. I always felt it was either him or me. I'll let you decide who walked or slithered away from those unhappy chance encounters...

"REJOICE WITH THOSE WHO REJOICE.

– *Romans 12:15*

MY DUCK DYNASTY NEIGHBORS

It's true. I grew up in West Monroe, Louisiana with the Duck Dynasty clan. It's not like we were hunting buddies or spent time racing our four-wheel drives down in the swampy mud holes, but we came from the same quiet little town, graduated from the same high school and grew up with the same slow-moving Southern culture. Momma still lives in our 50-year-old family home just on the other side of the woods from the place where Korie's grandparents lived. When I didn't have time to go into the deep woods along the Tupawek bayou, I enjoyed a short hike upstream along the little creek to the small lake behind their home. Sometimes I fished in the pond but never with much success. It was always more fun to throw rocks and try to reach their manicured backyard where it dipped down to the water. One summer they drained the pond completely to rid it of an overgrowth of duckweed and give it a new birth. A sturdy motor pumped thousands of gallons of green water across the road and into the creek. When the water was all gone the mushy ground revealed a sunken boat, lost fishing lures and rotten stumps. It made me think of Judgment Day when everything hidden will be brought to light. The hot summer sun baked the ground until it was firm enough to walk upon and when the snakes cleared out with the receding water I could wander around behind their house and admire their classy landscaping.

Long before the riches of Duck Dynasty, Korie's family, the Howards, enjoyed many business achievements. The Howard brothers started a discount chain similar to Wal-Mart that spread across the Gulf Coast. My personal favorite was Howard Griffin Land of Toys. A boat salesroom the rest of the year, it transformed into the most enchanting Christmas wonderland every November. The local television station ran an ad with an unforgettable jingle, "Howard Griffin Land O Toys/ loads of fun for girls and boys/ bring the kids and look around/the biggest toy deal in the town." Okay, it's not Shakespeare, but I'd bet my best hunting dog that every North Louisiana kid from the '70 can still sing it with a sparkle in their eyes. Inspired by the catchy Christmas jingle, my folks took me down to the river for a good look at the Land O Toys. I looked around with awe. Indeed, it was the best toy deal in the town, in the nation, in the world!

Everything the Howards touched seemed to turn the color of hundred-dollar bills. Howard Brothers discount stores expanded across the south, building bigger and bigger showrooms. But they were no match for Sam Walton. By the late 1980s Howards went out of business. The Howards however touched the publishing industry with their magic and created Howard Publishers. Working out of an office just a few blocks from the Robertsons' home church, White's Ferry Road Church of Christ, it quickly became one of the nation's most profitable Christian publishers. Always the shrewd businessmen, the Howards sold their publishing house to Simon and Shuster.

Like a marriage between the son and daughter of two European aristocracies, Willie and Korie's relationship brought together the redneck ruggedness of the Robertsons with the business acumen of the Howards. The combination was explosive.

Howard Publishers became the media arm of Duck Commander and the Howards' decades of business experience gave expert advice for capitalizing on opportunities in marketing.

After Duck Dynasty became the most watched show in cable TV history, I heard Alan Robertson speak one evening at a charity banquet in the West Monroe civic center. Momma and I sat and listened with fascination as he related some of the events of his life and the growth of the Duck Dynasty. It turned out that he and I graduated from West Monroe High School in 1982. His younger brothers like Jase and Willie came along after us, so our paths didn't cross and anyway--how can I say this delicately--back then the Robertson's were, well, they really were Rednecks!

The Robertson's lived way out south of I-20 behind the paper mill, somewhere in the swampy low-land that wasn't good for anything else but illegal trash dumping, filling huge junk yards full of rusty Fords and Chevys and mosquito breeding. Maybe that's one reason that part of West Monroe had so many honky-tonks as they were known, rickety little wooden buildings propped precariously on four or six cement blocks, filled with blaring country music of the most obnoxious kind and frequented by the sort of folks who inspired the country songs they were listening to while gulping cans of cheap beer.

Phil Robertson himself tells in his biography how he used to run one of those honky-tonks, not in West Monroe but out north in the deep woods and swamps on the border of Arkansas. After graduating from Louisiana Tech with a masters in English, he ran the bar but got into serious trouble with the law and, as he tells it, fled into the swamps as an outlaw.

I won't tell how Phil went from a half-wild outlaw to a settled family man and multi-millionaire, but interested folks find out more in any number of places. It wasn't an easy journey, nor one made all alone.

As a kid growing up in West Monroe I thought it would always be an obscure place, off the map and forgotten by the larger world. How *wrong* I was. When Phil did an interview where he spoke frankly about his beliefs regarding spirituality, sexuality and sin, journalists from around the world converged on North Louisiana. A friend of mine happened to be passing through West Monroe on vacation that week and said he and his family could barely find a place to stay because the hotels were packed with camera-toting journalists. West Monroe folks are still trying to adjust to the new fame, the swarms of tourists and curiosity seekers and the television crews. But truth be told, even though TV seems to make people larger than life, the Robertsons and other area folks are still just real people.

Late one evening my sister Vicki was doing some grocery shopping at the local market on Cypress Street. Suddenly down the aisle came Miss Kay Robertson. They smiled at one another and said hi, though they've never met before. My sister later joked that if she had been carrying her new Miss Kay Cookbook she got for Christmas, she would have asked for her autograph. Perhaps it was best she didn't have it; they simply said hi as neighbors in the corner grocery. In spite of all the hype, glitz, international fame and other TV stuff, that's what the Robertsons have always been and will continue to be; they are good neighbors in the community, not really larger than life, just part of it.

"THE PERILS OF DUCK HUNTING ARE
GREAT - ESPECIALLY FOR THE DUCK".

-- WALTER CRONKITE

LET'S GO HUNTIN'

We're getting pretty close to the end of the book and I still haven't mentioned a single thing about going hunting. Something's definitely wrong here. Louisiana wasn't nicknamed Sportsman's Paradise for its ski slopes and cliff rappelling. It will never be chosen for the Winter Olympics and not many people would dare to be found playing soccer on a real good ole' boy football field. The paradise part of the name mainly refers to the sport all rednecks learn before they can stand up straight. Hunting.

Daddy loved hunting for huckleberries and blackberries but he wasn't much interested in sitting for hours waiting for an unlucky buck to mosey by his stand or a duck to fly overhead. He enjoyed an occasional bowl of wild duck gumbo or fried squirrel, but not enough to go out and kill one. Daddy left it to my older buddy Butch to take on the job of teaching me about the finer points of real backwoods hunting.

The gun safety program at Boley gave me my first exposure to handling firearms. A couple years later Butch invited me to go duck hunting with him. He had several kinds of shotguns and let me borrow his 20-guage. I got my hunting license, feeling pretty big about myself, knowing that going hunting was the premier rite of passage for West Monroe boys, right up there next to playing football and dipping tobacco. Being good Christian folk, Momma and Daddy looked down very strongly on using tobacco and being on the light-weight side of average, I couldn't play football without the risk of a life-impairing injury. I definitely could, however, hoist a shotgun to my shoulder and blast the tarnation out of a duck or squirrel. I had come to my own personal rite of passage with great confidence that in spite of having a well-educated English teacher for a mother and a father who never drove a truck or used any tobacco or alcohol products, I could by virtue of mastering the hunter's firearm, enter the sublime ranks of redneckery.

My chances for success were dramatically increased by having my friend Butch, a true gentleman of the countryside, guide me in the ways of the backwoods. He not only hunted a wide range of water fowl, Butch could fire a softball over home plate like a major league pitcher. He carried our modest church softball team to some big wins and made a name for himself at the West Monroe softball fields behind the I-20 overpass. After church on Sunday evenings Butch and I often cruised over to the big city of Monroe in his customized baby-blue van for a barbeque sandwich with extra sauce and mayonnaise.

On the hunting day Butch came by the house before dawn. We both dressed warmly. The temperature hovered just below freezing, covering the field with snow-white frost and the smaller pools of water with a thin layer of clear ice. Dozens of hunters took to the woods and waterways that fine morning, turning the countryside into a battle zone. To get away from potentially crowded areas, we drove several miles into the backwoods, to a spot Butch had scoped out in previous hunting trips. The game of our choice that day was wood duck. These colorful and speedy little ducks nest high in the trees above the shallow flooded areas on the forest floor. Unlike duck hunting in a fixed position next to a bayou or lake, wood duck hunting requires lots of walking through the woodlands. Moving stiffly in our heavy boots, thick pants and several layers of shirts, we carried our shotguns into the woods as the first rays of dawn filtered through the leafless branches.

If any redneck is truly honest, he will have to admit that in this day and age hunting rarely has anything to do with survival. One of the most basic reasons for rising at an absurd hour, sloshing through mud and ice and silently gawking at the treetops is to experience the great outdoors up close and personal. Bagging a few squirrels or ducks is secondary, even for those rednecks whose wives or mothers prove to be exceptional cooks.

Butch walked on ahead and I tried to remember all of my hunter safety tips such as keep the chamber unloaded until you are ready to fire at game, walk with the gun pointing downward at all times and always know your hunting partner's location. Deer season was a few weeks away, so we weren't too worried about stray bullets flying through the woods. We climbed over fallen trees and through small creeks, going deeper and deeper into the backwoods to a place where Butch believed we would find some wood ducks.

The bright winter sunshine glittered on icy patches of water in a stand of hardwoods. It looked like an ideal spot for wood ducks. I loaded my 20-guage with shells filled with small lead beads, just the right size to reach the high-flying little wood ducks. Suddenly a high whistle and whir of rapidly beating wings skimmed over us. Butch tried not to shout when he said, "They're they go!" I watched two or three black shapes race overhead with incredible speed. Hitting one of these "top gun" fowl would not be easy.

With guns loaded and lifted up, we waited motionlessly, watching the tree tops for another fly over. Again the whistle came from nowhere followed by black shapes. *Boom, Boom.* Butch fired his gun and one of the ducks careened through the branches and fell to the ground.

"Hey, good shot," I said in genuine admiration.

"Look," he said with urgency.

This time I raised my gun and took aim just a little in front of the streak of black. The 20-guage kicked me hard in the shoulder when I pulled the trigger once and then again. To my great delight, the wood duck dropped down through the upper branches of the tall oaks. Its bold splash of colorful feathers make the male wood duck one of the prettiest. I suspect the ugly duckling was probably raised with a bunch of arrogant wood ducks who gloated over the gangly cygnet. I walked over to the plump duck lying in the shallow water. It was hot from flight. Admiring its lovely feathers, I imagined how good it would taste when Momma plunked it into a big pot of gumbo.

"Good shot," Butch said with a big smile.

"Thanks," I replied, my heart still racing from the thrill of the hunt.

"But that's not your limit yet."

"I know," I said, turning my ears and eyes back toward the sky. "So, let's get some more."

"NOW HIS LIFE IS FULL OF WONDER BUT
HIS HEART STILL KNOWS SOME FEAR
OF A SIMPLE THING HE CANNOT
COMPREHEND
WHY THEY TRY TO TEAR THE MOUNTAINS
DOWN TO BRING IN A COUPLE MORE
MORE PEOPLE, MORE SCARS UPON THE
LAND"

-- JOHN DENVER, ROCKY MTN HIGH

WILDCATS

Historically, Louisiana backwoods have harbored several wild cat species. The frisky bobcat grows about twice the size of a housecat. Any number of them still stalk small prey in the backwoods. Hunters can bag one bobcat a year, if they're lucky enough to see one of the elusive felines. They are masters of the forest, moving soundlessly on their padded feet in the shadows of the most remote backwoods. Many years ago at Camp Pollack I briefly saw a bobcat scurry under our cabin. My buddies and I shined our flashlights at the intriguing creature, making its eyes glow with a mixture of fear and curiosity. A thick coat of darkly speckled fur covered the bobcat and its large paws supported a sinewy frame. For a second we stood under the starry sky, each studying the other before it dashed into the forest and vanished.

The Louisiana backwoods have bred a peculiar controversy in recent decades. Any number of otherwise trustworthy eye-witnesses, including Momma and one of Daddy's brothers, claim to have seen a black panther in the wild. My uncle claimed that when he was a young man a black panther followed him home late one night after a church camp meeting. Allegedly he saw it padding along in the shadows, only a few feet away, as though it was stalking him and sizing him up for a late night snack. Momma still fervently defends her story of seeing a black panther in Louisiana during her childhood, in spite of all the evidence to the contrary regularly published by the Louisiana wildlife officials. In addition to the subjects of religion and politics, the question of black panthers is one best left undiscussed around our holiday dinner table.

Like the big black bear who showed up at a Ruston hotel uninvited, an occasional wild panther will follow a river or bayou corridor for hundreds of miles into Louisiana in search of territory and a mate. These big cats can grow over 200 pounds. Remember, that's 200 pounds of nothing but muscle, claws and teeth. These cats are lean, mean and seem to really enjoy eating meat. It's an interesting scientific fact that a vegetarian cougar has never been found in the wild. The vegetarian kind is arguably much rarer than the famed black panther. The average guy weighs about 170 pounds and is typically not as fit as the average 170 pound cougar. For this reason, cougars rarely find the welcome mat put out around most Louisiana communities. If they bother to stick their heads out of the woodland shadows, they will be quickly cornered and shot, with either a tranquilizer or something much worse.

Any community wanting to protect its people, especially the children, will justifiably respond to a wildcat sighting swiftly and sternly. Still, one can't help but feel that the backwoods have become a bit more impoverished by the absence of these noble beasts. No longer do their massive tracks in the soft dirt thrill the woodsman's heart and no more do they lead the way in culling the deer population.

After graduating from Louisiana Tech I moved away from my parents, married and had five boys. Work took us on adventures in backwoods far from West Monroe. We hiked high in the lofty Tien Shan Mountains between the former Soviet Union and China, explored rocky crevices on the island of Cyprus, backpacked in the Black Sea Mountains and looked for Robin Hood and his Merry Men under the beech and holly of England. However, whenever possible, we spent the holidays with Momma and Daddy, Pawpaw, Carrie and Vicki and their families and all the other relatives and friends.

One holiday, when the last two boys were still pretty small, I led them along my old childhood trails on a journey into the Tupawek woods. We donned our boots and coats, found some sturdy hiking sticks and tromped down the familiar hill behind the house. They laughed and chattered while constantly poking their sticks into the white sand piled along the creek bank.

I encouraged them to keep moving ahead and tried to increase their expectations for discovery. "Don't talk too much," I warned, "if you do it might scare away the wild animals. Granny said that deer have moved into the woods, and turkeys and lots of other things."

The thought of some large animal jumping out from behind a bush made them suddenly get very quiet. "Daddy," one of them said in a soft voice, "you think we'll find something?"

"Maybe. Look over here." At the edge of the forest I showed

them deer tracks scattered over the soft sand. "Who knows, maybe we'll even see a wild cat." I smiled when two sets of blue eyes opened very wide. "Now let's go, it's a long way in the woods."

The years since my childhood jaunts into the woods after school brought many changes to the terrain. The old barb-wire fence was rusted and most of the wooden fence posts sagged or dropped to the ground. A new house with a cement driveway occupied the wide field where Daddy brought us on our hike to the deep woods. I looked for the big oak tree near the field's edge where I gathered mistletoe each Christmas. Yes, it still stood there, displaying the cheery bunches of mistletoe, but the house and driveway blocked access to it. We turned away from the field and struck out along the wooded hillside nearer the creek.

"Here we are boys, this is a cedar," I said, breaking a dead branch from the faithful tree.

"That has a nice smell," my son said, sniffing at the purple wood again.

"Yes, you can take some with you to whittle it. But let's keep going, there's more to see."

Weaving our way between the slim ironwoods, we crunched through dead leaves and tried to avoid mud holes. Winter rains kept the creek full with water. I wanted to get across, so we followed it until we reached a large fallen tree trunk creating a natural bridge.

"Oh, this is fun," the boys said, scrambling onto the rough bark.

"Be careful, I don't want to fish you boys out of that cold water."

On the other side of the stream I led my sons right up the steep bank to a large stand of pines.

One of the boys paused. "Daddy, what's that noise?"

It didn't sound like a deer, bear, owl, hawk or turkey. A low growling sound made me curious and cautious. "I'm not sure," I said. "Let's go find out. Be careful."

We struggled along the steep hillside, moving briars and vines out of the way with our hiking sticks. The sound got louder. Just ahead I could see open sky where the pine forest used to make a dense canopy. We cautiously inched forward, hesitant to mistakenly trespass on someone's land. Two pairs of big blue eyes looked at me for reassurance. We pulled ourselves over the rim of the hill and scrambled up a pile of dead brush.

In front of us, moving back and forth with an annoying hum, a small backhoe busily pushed aside dead brush and dirt. There was no pine grove, no trails and hardly anything living. A cement road came to a dead end next to the woods. The backhoe buzzed around the end of the road, clearing up another empty lot in preparation for a cookie-cutter housing development.

For a moment my two boys and I crouched in the shadows of the brush pile, saying nothing and just watching the mechanized backhoe do its relentless job. I felt like someone from a long lost tribe looking out from under the forest cover at the arrival of the first settlers. Then I noticed it. The backhoe changed position and I had a clear view. There, written on its side, it said, *wildcat.*

"What is it Daddy?"

"Well, son," I said, trying to muster a chuckle, "I guess we found our wildcat. See, it's written on the side of that backhoe."

We lingered for a moment. I had seen enough. The boys and I worked our way back down the hill and across the creek. We made sure to take plenty of cedar. I pointed out the ironwood trees growing thick along the creek, explaining how they make some of the best hardwood walking sticks.

I don't resent people needing decent homes to live in and raise a family. The balance between protecting and using natural resources is very narrow. The real estate developer who hired that wildcat backhoe to clear out the Tupawek woods was hopefully just trying to provide folks with somewhere to live while making an honest living. Nothing wrong with that, at all.

Deep inside I have a special hope that helps me cope with watching the backwoods recede before the advance of backhoes and burning brush piles. My hope sustains me when I think of captured cougars and banished bears. I can carry on when I watch grand trees crash to the ground and delicate wildflowers vanish from the meadows. I believe that like everything else, all of nature has been affected by wrong choices people make. But I also believe that like everything else, nature will be completely renewed at a point in the future, perhaps not so distant. The ancient people called it the Day of the Lord. On that Day, the beauty of the backwoods, once marred and forsaken, will bloom anew, more glorious than ever.

BUT THEY THAT WAIT UPON THE LORD
SHALL RENEW THEIR STRENGTH; THEY
SHALL MOUNT UP WITH WINGS AS EAGLES;
THEY SHALL RUN, AND NOT BE WEARY;
AND THEY SHALL WALK, AND NOT FAINT.

-- ISAIAH 40:31

DADDY'S LAST HIKE

Old age slowed Daddy down but couldn't bring him to a standstill. He passed his 90th birthday with a good mind and toughness in his limbs. I reminded him that he used to call Pawpaw a tough old boot and encouraged him that he was now a tough old boot too. Far into his 80s Daddy wrote his own computer programming for cost-estimating in the paper container industry. He mowed and trimmed the big yard down to the bottom of the hill. His favorite plant was a luxuriant muscadine vine spread out in the trees next to the creek. The rich, moist loam deposited by annual floods made the muscadine, or wild grapes, plump up with sweet juice and tasty pulp.

In the early fall the cool weather turned the muscadine leaves into shades of gold and brought the plump fruit to the peak of ripeness. Daddy would often slowly trundle his way down the hill to the vine and give it a hard shake, bringing down dozens of ripe grapes. Sometimes he gathered up the muscadine grapes, stuffing his pant pockets full so Momma could transform them into a jar of delicious muscadine jelly. Other times he contented himself with blowing the dust off the grapes and popping them into his mouth for a tasty snack.

When Daddy turned 93 a routine medical checkup discovered a worrisome mole on his cheek. A specialist determined that the mole was melanoma and scheduled surgery. Unfortunately the post-op brought on a form of pneumonia that nearly took his life. For several weeks in the hospital the tough old boot struggling to survive and with the help of a very good wife and other caregivers, he eventually bounced back. But his fight aged him, so that he stooped lower and walked slower than ever.

Back at home Daddy soaked up the summer sunshine and found healing listening to the birds in the back yard. Little by little his strength returned and by the fall he could move around the yard without assistance.

With the return of his strength came the rise of his adventuresome spirit. One day, without telling anyone, he wandered down the hill to the muscadine vine growing at the bottom. It was a fine day and when he looked across the creek into the forest, he heard the unmistakable call of the wild. The little feeder creek that came down through a thick patch of underbrush piqued his curiosity. Where exactly did it come from? He walked past a flat area nearly surrounded by a horseshoe bend in the creek. When I was a kid he built me a miniature log cabin on that spot. I enjoyed it immensely until a couple of older boys knocked it partly down and flood waters carried away some of the logs. Daddy kept going and found a good place to cross the creek. Cold weather thinned out the foliage, giving him an easier path to follow. Step by slow step, he walked up the hill along the creek. He passed over a pebbly shallow pool, the same we crossed decades earlier on our first hike with him. Thick brambles and vines hung down over the creek bed. He stooped low, avoiding getting cut by the sharp thorns and twigs sticking out in all directions.

Forest sounds filled the air, but Daddy's ears weren't nearly strong enough to hear the subtle chirps and flutter of wings. He looked around. It was getting later in the day and he felt tired. He looked around again and felt a twinge of fear. Which way was home? The undergrowth hid everything from his sight. He knew he was close, but just couldn't say which was he should go. He slowly trudged forward, trying to find something familiar. His anxiety increased. No one knew where he was. He didn't tell anyone about his little adventure. What if he got lost? He kept walking.

Then to his surprise, he stepped into a clearing. Just beyond was a house and a road. Without realizing, Daddy went through the forest to the other side. He smiled, feeling somewhat relieved. But this meant he was a long walk from his house and he was quite fatigued by getting this far. Very slowly he shuffled to the edge of the road, hoping that he might get a second wind.

He stood there for a few moments, imaging the scolding he would get from Momma once he finally got home. He knew he was in trouble and had far exceeded the voice of prudence. What would he do now?

Maybe it was the expression of worry on his face, his drooping shoulders, or his dirty shoes, but something about him made the driver of an unfamiliar pickup truck slow down beside Daddy.

The friendly driver rolled down his window. "Howdy Sir, are you alright?"

Daddy's face gave the hint of an embarrassed smile. "Well, I've been walking in the woods and I guess I got a farther away from my house than I planned."

"Where do you live?"

"On the other side of these woods here. On Rainbow Drive."

"Could I offer you a ride, maybe? That seems like a pretty good walk to get back there." The man motioned. "Come on, it's no problem."

"I don't want to bother you," Daddy replied, ever reluctant to ask for help.

"Naw, it ain't no trouble a'tall. Just hop in, I'm goin' that way anyhow."

"I sure appreciate it young man," Daddy replied, climbing carefully into the cab.

"I'm glad to help."

They drove down the winding road until reaching the house. Daddy got out of the truck and thanked the stranger again. Momma came out to see the commotion.

"Where have you been!?" she asked in surprise. Daddy explained the whole episode; how he tried to take a short hike, got lost, ended up on the road and got a ride with the stranger in the pickup. Momma tried to contain herself, but wondered anxiously what antics Daddy would try to pull next.

Later I couldn't help but smile a little in spite of my concerns when Momma retold the story. All her anxious questions came tumbling out. What if Daddy had fallen in the woods and broken something? How would they have found him since he told no one he was going into the woods? What if he hadn't come out on the other side by the road? How would Daddy have gotten home in his exhausted condition if the kind Samaritan had not come by at just the right time? No one recognized the kind pickup driver or his truck; who was he anyway?

Like the impetuous Toad of *Wind in the Willows,* Daddy had to humbly accept his chastisement and promise to never again wander off on an adventure in the woods. He admitted it could have turned out much worse. He also listened soberly to Momma repeatedly tell her friends how God sent an angel in the form of a redneck pickup driver to rescue Daddy from his own recklessness.

They never learned the real identity of the young man who gave Daddy a ride home that afternoon. They felt a real debt of gratitude to him for taking the time to stop and help a worn-out woodsman. A small act of kindness possibly averted a big tragedy.

The next spring Daddy's pneumonia worsened. The tough old boot could walk no longer. He passed away in the summer. A couple of days before he died I strolled him in his wheelchair outside the nursing home. A storm was blowing over north Louisiana that day but it wasn't raining. Glancing up at the sky, I noticed some birds I hadn't seen for twenty years. Gliding on outstretched wings, some rare Mississippi kites went in lazy circles high above us. They looped in a circle and then turned back to do it again, enjoying the updraft of warm air rising from the pavement. Daddy couldn't lift his head far enough to see them. But they reminded me of a story he often told us children.

Once upon a time was a little Indian boy. His father was the chief and he lived with his people in the deep woods. The little boy loved spending time playing in the woods and pretending he was a great Indian warrior. One day he found an eagle in the woods. It couldn't fly because its wing was injured. The little boy took it home and nursed it back to health. When it was strong enough it would fly far in to the sky where he could hardly see it. But it always came back.

The day came the chief said to his son he must let the eagle be free. The boy didn't want to, but finally with tears in his eyes, he turned it loose and watched it soar away.

Not long afterwards the boy's father gave him a beautiful little canoe to ride in the stream. He was still sad about the eagle, but loved paddling in his canoe. He became a skilled paddler and one day went farther downstream than ever before. Without paying attention, the boy got caught in a strong current. It rushed him faster and faster downstream until he heard a terrible sound, the roar of a waterfall. Surely this would be the end. The boy silently pulled his paddle close to his side and waited for the inevitable.

All of a sudden a dark shadow fell over him. Great talons gently wrapped around his shoulders. Powerful wings lifted him up just as the canoe tumbled to destruction. His eagle friend had come back! It put him safely on dry land. Ever afterward, when walking in the deep wilderness or standing in a meadow, the boy could look in the sky and see a tiny black dot. A true friend, the eagle always watched over him.

Everything in our world is waiting. Things aren't like they will someday be. Something went wrong a long time ago and someday it will be put right. In the meantime, the backwoods offer people a beneficial alliance. Healing leaves sooth our sores. Silent swamps calm our questions. Ducks and deer feed our bellies. So, yeah, you could say that as a wobbly 93-year-old Daddy's last hike was foolhardy. But I think it was probably necessary for him, a sort of final rite of passage. He knew that eagles don't really swoop down and lift little boys from doomed canoe rides. But he knew that without the backwoods, people couldn't survive, much less thrive. His last hike was a chance to pay his last respects, to say good-bye to a very old friend. And I like to fancy that on that stormy summer day those Mississippi kites soaring over us had likewise come, along with me, to say their good-byes to a very dear, old friend.

ABOUT THE AUTHOR

Ron Coody graduated from West Monroe High School in 1982, along with several hundred ambitious Southerners, many of whom have ranged out far and wide across the US and the world since then. In 1986 he graduated from Louisiana Tech with a degree in microbiology. Interested in not only nature but the Source of nature, he earned a Master of Divinity from Anderson School of Theology and later a PhD in Intercultural Studies from Concordia Theological Seminary. He's especially proud of having taken his wife Jean and their five sons hiking in some of the most remote places on earth near the edge of Russia and China and in ancient Bible lands.